IN SEARCH
OF THE
SPIRIT

IN SEARCH OF THE SPIRIT

A Primer by Mary McDermott Shideler

A Ballantine/Epiphany Book
Ballantine Books • New York

A Ballantine/Epiphany Book

Permission to quote at length from the works of Charles Morgan has most graciously been granted by his son and literary executor, Roger Morgan.

"The Obedient" from "Epitaphs of the War" by Rudyard Kipling, Copyright 1919 by Rudyard Kipling from *Rudyard Kipling's Verse: Definitive Edition,* is reprinted by permission of the National Trust and Doubleday & Co., Inc. Permission to reprint throughout the British Commonwealth has been given by the National Trust for Places of Historic Interest or Natural Beauty, and Macmillan London Ltd.

Grateful acknowledgement is given to A.P. Watt Ltd. for permission granted by Miss D.E. Collins to quote the third stanza of G.K. Chesterton's "A Prayer in Darkness." The complete poem can be found in Louis Untermeyer, *Modern American Poetry, Modern British Poetry: Combined Edition* (New York: Harcourt, Brace & Company, 1930).

Library of Congress Cataloging in Publication Data

Shideler, Mary McDermott.
   In search of the spirit.

   Bibliography: p. 246
   1. Spiritual life.   I. Title.
BV4501.2.S4384   1985   248.3   84-24222
ISBN 0-345-32107-3

Manufactured in the United States of America
Text design by Holly Johnson

First Edition: December 1985

10 9 8 7 6 5 4 3 2 1

To
Thomas O. Mitchell
with my enduring gratitude
and affection

CONTENTS

PROLOGUE

> . . . *from outward forms to win*
> *The passion and the life, whose fountains are*
> *within.*

> Samuel Taylor Coleridge
> *"Dejection: An Ode"*

I have called this book a primer as a way of making clear not only what it is, but also what it is not intended to be.

It is not a scholarly analysis or historical conspectus of the spiritual life. It is not a textbook with instructions to be followed in a designated order, with an exhaustive and detailed catalogue of types of prayer, and summarizing data on the results of prayer with charts and graphs. It is not a devotional manual or a book of rules. It is meant primarily not for the experienced or the adept, but for novices, especially for those who simply do not know what to do with certain uneasy stirrings within them or flashes of illumination from without. It contains not prescriptions but suggestions, including notes on preconditions, enablements, impediments, dangers, possibilities, and theological implications. It is a sharing of many ways of spiritual development, not a course of instruction.

I shall be using the term "novitiate" for the period between our first spiritual awakening and our commitment to a particular spiritual tradition such as Christianity or Buddhism or Judaism, or to a particular set of practices such as meditation, yoga, or T'ai Chi Chu'an. The novitiate is a time for exploring the domain of spirituality by reading as widely, investigating as thoroughly, and reflecting as deeply as our circumstances permit.

Almost certainly we were brought up in some tradition, be it one of the "great religions", or free-thinking or atheism or whatever, and characteristically, though not universally, at some time we have rejected our childish understanding of it. Our rejection may have been so complete that from then on we submerged ourselves in the mundane, writing off everything that might lead us beyond it. Or there may have remained some vestiges of longing that the mundane cannot assuage. Years—possibly much of a lifetime—may elapse before we take that longing seriously enough to follow through on it. That matters very little. Essentially, all it means is that the late beginner has more to work with, not only more burdensome habits of thought and living, but also richer experience. In contrast, the early beginner is likely to be more flexible and more venturesome. Neither is handicapped; they simply have different assets and liabilities that balance each other out.

My inquiries into the life of the spirit have been long, rambling, sporadic, and for the most part solitary. With only occasional exceptions, the books I have read on the subject, the lectures and sermons I have heard, and the discussions I have participated in, have not spoken to my condition, usually for one or more of three reasons. They presupposed commitment to a theological position or psychological theory that I did not share. Or they failed to provide any means by which I could determine whether I were ready to undertake what the writers or speakers were advising. Or they made no allowance for individual differences in temperament, natural abilities, concerns, and circumstances. For example, Evelyn Underhill, in her classic book *Mysticism*, makes both psychological and theological assumptions which I could not accept at the time when I most needed a survey of the field, and some of them are still alien to me. C. S. Lewis's *Letters to Malcolm: Chiefly on Prayer* presupposes that the reader already knows what prayer is and has had some experience with its various forms. At least one highly praised spiritual manual maintains that the only way spiritual life can begin is with a sense of sin, the conviction that one is a sinner, for which I find no evidence in history or my own observation. Others lay down as the sine qua non a "religious experience" such as that of "being born again" or a mystical vision.

For a number of years, I believed that I was unique in my unresponsiveness to such guides. For even more years, I believed that the fault lay in my stupidity or willfulness or hardness of heart. As I discovered others who shared my disabilities, however, eventually I reached the conclusion that the root of my difficulty lay in the fact that I had been taught *how* to pray—that is, one or two techniques—but not how to *pray*, what prayer is all about. Thus I had the letter without the spirit. Later I had the spirit without the letter, and so was deprived of resources that would have helped me immeasurably if I had known about them.

For example, as a child, I took prayer to be kneeling beside my bed and reciting "Now I lay me down to sleep", upgraded after a while to the Lord's Prayer. As an adult, I was instructed that prayer is conversation with God, as natural and easy as talking with a friend and listening to him. But neither formal nor informal discourse of that kind proved adequate for my needs or confirmed my tentative experiences. The definition of prayer as "the soul's sincere desire, uttered or unexpressed",[1] gave me nothing that I could practise at will, much less direct. The innumerable variations on the theme that prayer is a special type of self-examination or self-help convinced me only that those who so define it are not talking about what I was searching for, and now and again finding. For me, meditation neither substituted for nor issued in prayer. And so it was with a multitude of other definitions and portrayals that had been proposed to me.

There are many of us who want to pray, but our efforts are stillborn because we do not really know what we are supposed to be doing. Even though we may be acquainted with a variety of techniques, we do not understand what different functions those techniques are supposed to perform or what results we can expect to achieve with them. Or habit or ignorance restricts us to one or two methods, so that our potential for spiritual growth is limited.

Behind that specific disability lies a more general one: the mood of "scientific" materialism in which most of us have been nurtured, and which still surrounds us. We have been taught to be so wary of any "motions of the spirit" that we distrust its leading. Consequently, many of us who are spiritually-minded are half-starved without knowing it, half-sick but convinced that we are healthy, aching but sure that the pain is natural to human beings—and irremediable.

Moreover, none of the beginners I have known—including myself—has been able to find a person trained in spiritual direction to whom we could go for guidance, encouragement, and correction. And the prayer groups we have been acquainted with were not equipped to help us with our particular problems as beginners. Whatever their value for others, in them we found ourselves blocked or puzzled or obscurely repelled.

Much of what I have learned about the spiritual life has come through reading, though for the most part not from books concerned with prayer or the devotional life as such. My principal resources have been imaginative works—fiction and poetry—and next in importance, more or less technical studies in fields such as theology, history, biography, and in one significant case, literary criticism.[2] Some of the rest I have learned from occasional conversation and correspondence with the rare friends with whom I could discuss these achingly intimate affairs, but I have learned most from experimenting. By experimenting,

5

I do not mean "running experiments" as scientists do but simply trying out practices to see if they worked for me. Many of them did not. But I did learn from this procedure, though very slowly, one thing of extreme importance: first to develop and then to trust my own sense of the fitness of things and of how I fit in with them.

No single book on the spiritual life—certainly not this one!—will meet all needs or answer every question. It is open to debate whether any book on that subject can do more than make explicit what the reader dimly perceives already but cannot yet formulate for himself. Until competent spiritual directors become widely and readily accessible, however, we must depend heavily upon books. And books do have undeniable virtues. A book can be read in solitude, at one's own pace. It is infinitely patient, neither tiring of repetition, nor demanding that we adjust our schedules to its convenience, nor resenting our neglect. In its company we do not have to wear a mask or fear that we shall be patronized, or even condemned, when we inwardly cry "No!" or "Yes!"

This last point is of particular moment because the life of the spirit is almost always, I believe, secret in its earliest stages. Instinctively we hide from others the preliminary stirrings of the spirit within us or our first visions of the glory, even when we recognize what they are, which is not always the case. We tend to feel ashamed of them—not a surprising reaction within a society which has lost sight of the distinction between modesty and shame, lumping them together as unnatural restraints upon the free development of individuality. Decrying the "hypocrisies and tragic repressions" of our forebears, many people today boast that they have nothing to conceal. Defining all human functions as legitimate, if not in themselves good, they insist that it is legitimate, if not positively good, to perform them all in public.

No doubt some of our predecessors were hag-ridden by artificial prescriptions and prohibitions. But some of them possessed a sensitivity to rich and subtle delights that cannot be fully savored in the midst of a crowd, to delicate colors that are washed out by television lights, to forms of life that need quietness in order to grow. Is it shame that causes the seedling to wither in the glare of the summer sun? Is the butterfly repressed during the time before it is ready to emerge from its chrysalis? Is it hypocrisy for the cat to seek a dark and hidden place to deliver her young?

The reluctance that we feel in speaking of our spiritual life may be no more than the shield with which we protect our personal growing edges from destruction by cruel or careless or unskillful handling, and ensure their nourishment, as the child is sheltered and nourished in the womb. Some things must be concealed at certain times, not because they are ugly or wrong, but because they are precious and fragile. The forms of modesty can be cultural artifacts, and so false; the impulse toward modesty is a spontaneous defense against violation.

This early secretiveness is intensified by the fact that although there are abundant reports from the spiritually mature detailing what the life of the spirit, or life in the spirit, is like, there is none that I know of devoted to what might be called "early apprenticeship": how to move from the first inklings of spirituality to a fair degree of understanding, skill, and confidence.

In reading, we preserve that modesty which is necessary for some stages of personal and spiritual development, while opening ourselves to illumination, reassurance, and counsel—to spiritual direction—with or without an immediately present director. But although books do foster creative solitude, they do not effectively guard against isolation, and isolation circumscribes the interactions that create and sustain us as persons. Only in a limited sense can a book listen or talk back, and only in one important way does it help to release us from isolation: by providing us with a set of words—and, even more valuable, of concepts—for our use when openness becomes appropriate and it is possible for us to enter a more direct interchange with other persons.

This is not to decry the value of wise spiritual directors, soul friends, and formal or informal prayer groups, as they become available. All of us go through times when we need reassurance that we are (or are not) on the way that is right for us, or guidance on how to handle a particular spiritual problem. Companionship in our spiritual endeavors is beyond price. But we must choose carefully among those who offer themselves as mentors or companions, or to whom we offer ourselves, and we must be prepared to part company if they prove unsuitable for our particular journey.

Although I am writing from within the Christian tradition and no doubt that commitment will continually be apparent, nothing I say here has been included with the aim of persuading anyone to follow the path that I took. Now and again I shall indicate what special opportunities and responsibilities lie before the person who is committed to Christianity, but the life of the spirit is not tied to any one religious tradition, theology, ethic, or form of worship. My immediate concern is not so much with what we worship as with whether we worship at all, in the belief that it is through the act of praying that we discover what—or whom—we are approaching when we pray.

Much of what we discover, of course, will depend upon *how* we pray. It may be that in the end there is some one best way of praying for everyone: meditative, contemplative, intercessory, mystical, liturgical, or other. Even if this be so—and I, for one, believe it is not so—at the beginning we shall do well not to narrow our experience and limit our techniques by establishing *a priori* norms. Here is an ideal opportunity to explore as widely as our individual natures and circumstances permit, within the bounds of prudence. Extreme ascetic practices like prolonged fasting or wearing garments that irritate or injure the body are emphatically not to be undertaken by novices, and probably never except under professional direction. As beginners, we do not yet know the range of possibilities for developing spiritually, or our own capacities and limits. Now is the time to try different ways of praying, and to experiment with different ways of relating ourselves as spiritual beings not only to the ultimate, but also to the mundane world in which we live our daily lives.

At times I have wished that I could find or invent a word other than "spirit" to designate the realm of thought, experience, and action that includes the perception of holiness, the response of wonder, the impulse toward repentance, and the invasion by a transcendant Other. On the whole, I think it is just as well that I have failed in the attempt. The terms "spirit" and "spiritual" may be philosophically indefensible and popularly corrupt, but they tie us to our past, and thereby open the way for us to learn from those who have gone before us, and who can give us great riches when we are ready to receive them. Further, use of the traditional language constitutes an invaluable discipline. As Charles Morgan writes, "Let us use the great words still—God, Satan, heaven, hell—lest for want of them we babble arrogantly of our toys."[3]

In this context, however, I have chosen not to use those traditional terms. "Satan, heaven, and hell" do not arise. And "God" has too many associations for many of us, associations which tend to impose constraints upon our experience when they do not contradict it. Not infrequently, our spiritual experience shatters our theological preconceptions: the ultimate (which perhaps we may come to name God, or perhaps not) is incredibly more and other than we had imagined, as our actual falling in love is more and other than what we had heard described before it happened to us.

Moreover, many persons who sense an urging beyond the mundane do not believe in any deity, and some are alienated by that notion. Except in special cases, therefore, I shall use instead two terms interchangeably, terms that are as noncommittal as any I could find: "the ultimate" and "the transcendent", and I am taking them as adjectives rather than as nouns. Anyone who wishes to be more specific—e.g., "the ultimate reality", "a transcendent God"—is free

10

to do so. Those who prefer to reserve their commitment are equally free.

My general procedure will be to describe the life of the spirit, using for the most part as simple and commonplace illustrations as I can devise, without trying to define either "spirit" or "spiritual" in formal terms. This much, however, can be said in advance: that in the sense I am using the phrase, "spiritual life" is not separate from physical and intellectual life, or antagonistic to nature (even human nature), or merely a word for certain natural functions such as aspiration or conscious intention. Such topics as mysticism, faith healing, speaking with tongues, and other special aspects of spirituality will not be mentioned at all. Examination of those subjects belongs to a more advanced study than this one.

Two notes on terminology are in order. First, I am using the word "prayer" in a sense broader than the dictionary definitions of it as entreating, supplicating, petitioning, and offering. There seems to be no word in English that covers not only those activities but also meditation, contemplation, "conversation with God", and various other forms of interaction with the ultimate. Consequently I have chosen to extend the meaning of the common word rather than to seek for an uncommon one from Greek or Latin or some other language.

Second, it is only within very recent years that the pronoun "he" and the noun "man" have been taken by anyone as exclusively masculine in their reference. Before that, through the whole development of the English language, "he" and "man" were universally understood either as inclusively generic like the

Greek *anthropos* and the Latin *homo*, or as exclusively masculine as the Greek *aner* (genitive *andros*) and the Latin *vir*, their meaning being clear from the context. "She" and "woman", however, have always been exclusively feminine. Faced with the choice between any of the "he and/or she" forms which are currently fashionable but awkward in whatever variation, and the generic "he" and "man", I have chosen the latter, trusting the intelligence and good will of my readers to interpret them as non-sexist. Therefore every use of the generic "he" should be taken as followed by the parenthetical "or she or it or they, this to be understood throughout", and the equivalent for "man".

I began writing this book some twenty years ago, often referring to notes that I had kept during the ten years before that. The first draft was nearly finished when I succumbed to external pressures and reluctantly abandoned it, returning only when I was driven back to it by an inward necessity. It has gone through many drafts since then. I cannot emphasize too strongly that it is a *primer*, and that I have neither the experience nor the wisdom for anything more advanced. In the field of education, however, it has been discovered and well tested in elementary schools that in some cases, children learn faster by sharing with their peers than from instruction by highly trained adults. Spiritually, I am still in the early grades, but for just that reason I may appreciate more keenly the difficulties peculiar to beginners.

I am grateful beyond measure to a number of persons who have expanded my horizon, sharpened my vision, and reproved my aberrations. Chief among those whom I have known only through books are

Charles Morgan, Dorothy L. Sayers, Charles Williams, C. S. Lewis, and G. K. Chesterton. Among those whom I have had the privilege of knowing personally, I want to mention especially the late Robert B. MacLeod, Kathryn Benbrook Lapp, and Henry Burton Sharman, and the following who are still among the living: Janet Bailey, Jan Vanderburgh, Peter G. Ossorio, Dorothy Macy, Jr., M.D., Joseph Sittler, Lucile Long Hair, the monks and nuns of the Spiritual Life Institute, Michelle Rapkin of Ballantine/Epiphany Books, my editor Julie Garriott, and finally, the friend to whom this book is dedicated, whose encouragement led me to rewrite and finish it, and whose critiques have been invaluable.

PART ONE

A Beginning

Not only then has each man his individual relation to God, but each man has his peculiar relation to God. . . . Hence he can worship God as no man else can worship him,—can understand God as no man else can understand him. This or that man may understand God more, may understand God better than he, but no other man can understand God as he understands him. . . . From this it follows that there is a chamber . . . in God himself, into which none can enter but the one, the individual, the peculiar man,—out of which chamber that man has to bring revelation and strength for his brethren. This is that for which he was made—to reveal the secret things of the Father.

George MacDonald
Unspoken Sermons

CHAPTER ONE

The Awakening

*I saw well why the gods do not speak to us openly,
nor let us answer. . . . How can they meet us face
to face till we have faces?*

C. S. Lewis
Till We Have Faces

Among the myriad ways of spiritual awakening, two
stand out as most frequently referred to: the pervasive
sense of an absence, and the awareness of a presence;
and these can be roughly correlated with something
happening within us and something happening to us.

The sense of absence often takes the form of a continuing dissatisfaction with what we are and are doing,
an impression of something missing, incomplete, in-

adequate, a lack or distortion of order and meaning. This may be the more poignant for those occasional moments of delight or repose when we seem to glimpse a completion, an adequacy, a fulfilment, that includes ourselves. For a time we may attribute our uneasiness to circumstantial or psychological factors: "If only I were married … if only I had a different job … if only I lived somewhere else … if only I had not had an unhappy childhood … if only I weren't afraid". Yet the desolation can also afflict those who are neither situationally nor psychologically in trouble: "I have everything that I could want but it isn't enough". or "I don't have what I want, but even if I did, it wouldn't be enough. That isn't the sort of thing I *really* want".

But we don't know what we *really* want, so we don't know where to look.

If we confide our distress to someone else, the chances are that we shall be answered in one of three ways. The first: you need more of what you already have. The second: you need what *I* already have. The third: this is the natural state of persons, and it is irremediable. A person who accepts the first answer knows what to do or can easily find out. Self-help resources abound in every bookstore and library. Support groups flourish. A person who accepts the second answer will find prophets, gurus, evangelists of almost every stripe on almost every corner. One who accepts the third has no alternative except to learn endurance in his despair because it is a counsel of despair.

Another possible answer deserves more attention than it is usually given: to look in our own experience, past and present, for what—in the Quaker phrase—

speaks to our condition and follow that lead. With what persons—books—music—activities—are we most at home? What events have lightened our darkness, if only briefly? When are we most completely ourselves? What touches us most poignantly, moves us most deeply? The half-hour alone when we let everything drop away into silence? The presence or memory of a person whose serenity is infectious? A line of poetry or a melody that acts as a talisman? A pain that is somehow like the pain of a healing wound, and so is welcome?

For the healing of the body, we take for granted that one person needs a cast for a broken bone, another an antibiotic, another a nutritional program. For the healing of spiritual emptiness, all too often we suppose that a single remedy will be effective for everyone. "Read this book ... engage faithfully in these spiritual exercises ... participate in social or political or economic reform ... only believe in this that or the other ... and you will be filled." Almost anything will work for some people; our problem is to identify what works for *us*, and there is no way to find that out except by observing what speaks to *our* condition. And we begin that by following out whatever hints we have been given in the past.

Because we need all the help we can get, we shall, of course, be open to suggestions from many sources. But also, if we are wise, we shall not be so gullible as to change our way of living radically while we are still new in the life of the spirit. That time may come. Later in our spiritual journey we may be called to forsake our customary associates and occupations in favor of new ones. Or we may instead be called to continue with them but to see them in a new light—which is in fact equally radical, although less conspicuous.

A more subtle temptation is to take as unquestionable the word of those who say, "If you don't obtain these results from this program, it's your own fault. You haven't done it right—or you haven't kept at it long enough. You haven't given it a fair trial". But what constitutes a fair trial? A week or a lifetime? That is where we must listen to our selves, because sooner or later our selves will tell us, "This is not for me".

Or our selves may tell us, "This *is* for me", an intuition or insight which is often associated with the sense of a presence, and may constitute the first step in our spiritual awakening, or a second step following emptiness. Either way, it is best approached through the common, mundane experience of surprise, as natural as a child's astonishment at an unexpected treat, as spontaneous as an adult's reaction to a sudden reversal of his expectations. Something—whether delightful or horrifying or merely unforeseen, and whether subtle or spectacular—intervenes to shake us out of our usual patterns of thought and response, and into new ones.

Generally we respond to what surprises us in one of three ways: a movement to withdraw; a movement to investigate or to engage ourselves, either by merely inquiring or by intervening; or a cessation of movement in wonder, amazement, awe. An unusual noise in the street outside my window interrupts my train of thought. It frightens me: I jump back into the room to get as far away from it as possible. Or it lures me into the second type of response: I approach the window in curiosity. What caused the sound? How can I find out? What should I do about it, if anything? A strangely beautiful or ominous sound might evoke the third response: a rapt attention to the sound itself, regardless of its meaning or demands.

The response of surprise does not usually endure for more than a moment. And it is likely to be complex. Almost simultaneously we step back and then forward, or stop short while we take in the shock and then advance or retreat. An habitual tendency toward one response or the other, however, leads to quite different consequences. The practice of armoring ourselves against surprise may lead eventually to an apathy not far removed from personal death. An emphasis upon approaching what surprises us, in order to inquire into or control or possess it, can lead to science and technology, scholarship, and other productive enterprises. The stress upon wonder may produce the receptivity out of which worship grows, and—upon occasion—theology and the arts.

Flight, curiosity, wonder. The movement away from the situation, ignoring or dismissing or rejecting it. The movement of approach, to participate, to probe, or perhaps to master it. The cessation of movement as we yield to the event, not questioning or defining, but opening ourselves to whatever it has to give.

Within certain groups it is considered a weakness, a disgrace, to be astonished by anything. The mature person, they hold, has experienced so much that nothing can surprise him any more. According to them, to be mature is to be blasé, and only the childishly naïve succumb to the urge for exploring deeply into the unknown or for worshipping a mystery. The mood of these sophisticates may be cynical or stoical or fearful or merely bored; whichever predominates, the person implicitly assumes mastery over himself and the world. He will not allow himself to be surprised; he will not allow life to utter surprises. He builds himself an impregnable fortress and retires within it.

To be incapable of surprise is to be not fully a person. Unless we allow *something* to startle or astonish or shock us, we shall be too inert even to start upon the way of the spirit. Initially it seems not to matter much what it is that surprises us: a thing of glory or dread, the exotic or the commonplace, a mathematical equation or the prospect of death, the sense of guilt or an ecstatic vision. It is of primary importance—again, initially—that we differentiate between the occasions when we are honestly and spontaneously surprised, and those where we pretend to ourselves that our curiosity or wonder has been aroused.

Merely to identify what deeply shocks or surprises us can be difficult if not painful. The center that is touched by surprise is exquisitely sensitive, and we may not be able to admit, even inwardly, that we are indeed surprised without stripping away protective crusts that we have been fashioning for years. For example, we have been told repeatedly and with immense authority that we ought to be astonished by human wickedness, awed by the beauty of the Grand Canyon of the Colorado, and inquisitive about scientific discoveries, until now we are ashamed to admit even to ourselves that none of these touch us at all. Worse, we are ashamed to admit that the authentic shock of personal surprise comes to us not through such publicly approved channels, but in less reputable and more individual ways.

To illustrate from my own experience: few incidents have been more determinative for my spiritual growth than a question that I was asked when I was five or six: "Do you believe in fairies?" I was well aware that a child of my years ought to answer No, but I could not say it, and sixty years later I still quiver at the shock of realizing, in that moment, the discrepancy between what my questioner and everyone else judged that I ought to be, and what I was.

While walking through a forest not long ago, impulsively I picked up a small stone, an ordinary pebble about the size of a walnut. As I stood holding it, the marvel of its weight broke upon me. How silly it sounds—how silly it was—for a person of my advanced age to be amazed not only that a stone has weight, but also that this one had no more and no less than I expected. Parts of Benjamin Britten's "Hymn to Saint Cecilia" invariably move me to tears although I know it well, having once belonged to a choir that sang it. I can confess that response without undue discomfort because the music is praised by competent critics, and because those who read what I am writing are far enough removed from my presence that the confession becomes depersonalized. But for many years I would not admit that the writings of Charles Morgan reached me at a depth that no other author did, because nobody I knew had ever heard of him, and therefore I concluded—mistakenly—that I must be foolishly uncritical to respond so strongly to his work.

Other admissions I will not confide even to the comparatively antiseptic medium of print, but all these responses contain a vital element of surprise. My memory or anticipation is blurred compared with the poignancy of my encounters with them, so that when

I re-read the books or hear the music again, the reality strikes me with fresh power.

Some of my secret reactions contradict my good opinion of myself, showing me to be more simple-minded or unstable than I like to think of myself as being. For just this reason, however, they are heartening. My honest feeling about Morgan's books was not clouded by the conjecture that it was molded by someone else's opinion. When my spontaneous reaction contravenes the accepted social standards, or jeopardizes my self-esteem, I can be reasonably sure it is authentic, and that it does not represent self-deception in the form of wish-fulfilment or an urge toward conformity. The person who is thus revealed may not be admirable, but is indubitably me.

We do not undertake the discipline of identifying what surprises us in order to attain self-knowledge, although that may come as a by-product. What we are after now is a touchstone by which we can recognize what in the world speaks to our condition. We have been told so often what we ought to think and how we ought to feel that often our authentic personal responses are buried under layer upon layer of conventional husk. We are upheld by an external shell rather than by an internal skeleton. Consequently our relations with the world and the people around us tend to be falsified, except for those few that penetrate to waken the person within, no matter if they are officially approved like a death, or ridiculous like holding a pebble in the hand.

All societies inhibit curiosity and wonder to some degree, as inevitable concomitants to establishing the social structures designed to secure us against chaos.

In Western civilization, where curiosity has issued in a scientific culture, a question about how a so-called witch-doctor can kill or heal from a distance is likely to be dismissed with a curt "It's all the power of suggestion"—a rejoinder which at once fails to answer the question ("the power of suggestion" is scarcely less mysterious), and curtails in all but the hardiest any zeal to investigate the phenomenon. A child who asks about fairies or angels is fortunate if his curiosity is met with an answer more mind-stretching than "There are no such things".

In those great cultures, notably Asian and African, where the natural impulses toward awe and adoration are not disparaged, the equally natural impulse of curiosity is sometimes met with the courteous insistence that the questioning intellect be left outside the sacred precincts. Only a few, in any culture, have the imaginative vitality to stray very far beyond their cultural limits, or the courage to do so.

If we set forth grimly determined that the world shall surprise us, we shall be trying to manipulate the world, to compel its obedience to our demand for a certain kind of experience. So doing, we shall find no more than we expect, and nothing other than the little we can foresee on the basis of our past. All we can properly do is to be ready for the surprises when they come, and to recognize what they are: voices from outside ourselves which, for whatever reason and in whatever way, speak directly to us as unique persons.

We shall not identify what surprisingly speaks to us in an afternoon of introspection or years of psychotherapy. Indeed, neither self-examination nor professional counselling may be required at all—or either or both may be. No one procedure will be suitable for all persons: we are too varied in our capacities and our levels of development. Thus in the early stages of spirituality, it is usually out of place to inquire what events in our past have led us to respond positively to one stimulus and negatively to another. How we became what we are can be a fascinating archeological enterprise, but almost certainly it is not relevant to our initial task, even though it may become not only relevant, but imperative, later on. Or it may not.

The most urgent task for many of us is that we should turn our gaze outward, looking for what the world contains for our quickening rather than to observe ourselves in the process of responding—to scour the countryside for food rather than to observe in ourselves the process of digesting. What in the world enlivens us? Where do we find sustenance? Authorities cry, "Lo, here! Lo, there!" The feasts they spread may satisfy a thousand others, but leave us starving. The lion and the lamb need different kinds of food. The sparrow and the whale cannot feed from the same dish.

Neither praise nor blame attaches to being a lion instead of a lamb. The sparrow is not intrinsically higher or lower in the scheme of creation than the whale. But not to know in general which we are, and not to accept what we are, can be ruinous. We become whales trying to fly, or lions seeking to be vegetarians. Our reactions to the world—the kinds and degrees of our curiosity and wonder and withdrawal—indicate that we are childish or antiquated or cowardly or eccentric? Very well, we are childish, antiquated, cowardly, or eccentric, without apology and without conceit—though also without complacency.

It may not be prudent to reveal our essential selves

to other persons, but within ourselves we shall not pretend that the liturgy they love has any meaning for us, if it does not, or that their talisman will be effective for us if it is not. Nor shall we ingenuously suppose that the word that entrances us will be audible or intelligible to them. Even with such an apparently innocuous reaction as simple surprise, it is sometimes opportune and sometimes a virtue to hide the expression of our authentic feelings or pretend what we do not feel. By all means let us act startled not only the first, but also the fifth time that the youngster shows off his Jack-in-the-box, and possibly even the fiftieth. And let us cherish in secret those fragile intimations which others would misunderstand or deride, or that are not yet mature enough to survive our exposing them.

We do not learn who we are by looking directly at ourselves or by examining what we think or how we behave. Nor do we discover ourselves by asking others their opinion of us: how our friend or lover or acquaintance or enemy appraises us will be no more than the froth on the wave. Still less do we look for the way in which they and the rest of the world react to our presence: their responses are governed by countless factors in addition to who and what we are. Instead, who we are corresponds to our place in the world. It is a summary formulation of all our relationships, which we apprehend principally by observing what the world asks from us, denies to us, and says to us in many circumstances.

So, for example, if we enjoy reading more than competitive games like chess, and imaginative fiction more than biographies, it is generally more fruitful to gratify our unforced enthusiasm than to investigate why we prefer one to the other, or to try dutifully to learn those games and read those biographies in the hope that when we have played or read them enough, we shall find them interesting. If instead we admit quite simply that we are captivated by this but not by that, and then follow where our captor leads us, we are far more likely to discover who or what has captured us, and thereby what terms are appropriate for discovering who we are.

But many voices call us. Many masters enthrall us to some degree. We are intellectually stimulated by one summons and emotionally moved by another. Duty conflicts with inclination. What we want collides with what others want from us. We must choose which to obey, not only once but repeatedly, and not only at one depth of our existence but at many depths.

To each particular person the world speaks a different, particular word and calls for a different, particular response. To none is it silent, because everything that exists is fatefully involved with every other thing. Their fate depends directly or indirectly on what we do and ours upon what they do. What we—individually and particularly—should answer to the world's demands, invitations, and pleas, we learn by applying the touchstone of what speaks to our condition, what rings true to us. What in particular surprises *us*? What in particular resists and supports *us*? What particular voice pierces through *our* conventionality? What accents stir *our* blood? With what companions are *we* most truly ourselves? The test is not infallible, but it is indicative, and if in using it we make mistakes, at least they are our own mistakes and therefore potentially creative errors.

When, in the life of the spirit, we permit others to

make our responses for us, as when we succumb to others' mandates about what we ought to do or be, or follow the crowd because it takes less effort—and is less dangerous—than thinking and acting for ourselves, we commit their mistakes and can learn nothing directly from the consequences. More accurately, we learn nothing except that if we capitulate to a word that does not reverberate in our own hearts, we diminish ourselves as persons. Indirectly we may learn from such submissions a good deal about the laws that inhibit growth and the futility of forcing persons into a prefabricated mold, but we gain no insight into what specific tendencies we most urgently need to guard against or encourage. From the errors we commit from within ourselves, however, we can garner a spiritual harvest that will nourish us: not the ethereal wisdom of generalities but the practical wisdom of living flesh and blood.

Thus I have conformed to fashion in the fear that my independence represented only a wish to show off. I have taken advice against my intuitive judgement because I had assigned to the person who gave it a position of authority over me. I have failed to carry through a promising train of thought when it headed in an unorthodox direction, and have spoken my mind at shamefully inappropriate times. These were *my* mistakes, exhibiting *my* failures of integrity or intelligence or courage or compassion, pointing up the defective ways in which *I* was relating myself to the world. Those lessons were precisely applicable to me.

When, however, I made the critical error of surrendering myself wholly to an authority of whatever kind—parent, spouse, political or social leader, psychological or religious arbiter—I learned much about those others' flaws and faults but little about my own. And by participating in the world primarily through that authority, I denied myself full personal participation and so, without ceasing to participate, corrupted my identity and jeopardized my integrity. Had I taken those authorities only as guides or mentors, I could have retained my identity and integrity, and benefited exceedingly from their admonitions. My mistake was in giving them an absolute authority.

In becoming spiritual persons, we embark on a process of education rather than what I shall call "formation". Despite the evidence from biographies and teachings of those generally accepted as archetypes of the religious life, from the Buddha to the Christ and from Confucius to Gandhi, the idea persists that the spiritual life has a prescribed structure to which the religious person is supposed to conform. Devotional literature is crammed with instructions for schooling the devout in habits of thought and behavior that are suitable for "religion", often—unfortunately—without reference to whether they are suitable for the individual religious person. If he cannot or will not undergo spiritual formation according to prescription, he is presumed to be incapable of progressing beyond the elementary levels of prayer and worship, and may be punished for disobedience.

There are those for whom subduing themselves to a predetermined style is natural and right. Their way is hallowed by tradition, but it is not for everyone, and this book was not written for them.

In contrast, education in the spirit is a matter of being liberated to develop our natural styles. The word "education" is derived from the Latin *educere*—

to lead out; in education, as contrasted with formation, we do not try to be "spiritual" and do not cultivate a "spiritual life", but we seek truth or God or the gods or love or beauty or whatever it is that we take to be ultimate. Nor do we try to make ourselves over, or to fit ourselves into a pattern, but to obey such intimations as we receive, and if those intimations lead us to contravene the ideal of the saint or the program of a given system, so much the worse for the ideal and the program.

Authenticity of style, whether in art or in life, does not result from trying to create an effect. It is a by-product of seeing with one's own eyes, working with one's own hands, and responding from one's own depths. Unquestionably some persons are called to forswear epicurean delights, sexual gratifications, close family ties and friendships, and satisfying personal achievements, for their spiritual maturation. Others are called instead to embrace them, either as stages on *their* way or as the consummation of their way. Whether such courses of action are forbidden to us as inappropriate, or permitted, or commanded is determined by the claim of the ultimate upon *us*. It has nothing to do with the claims of the ultimate upon anyone else. The goal of spirituality is neither conformity nor non-conformity, but obedience.

Most of us in the Western world, and many in the Asiatic and African worlds, have been trained from childhood to be individuals in societies, humans gathered into organizations. We have picked up along the way, as best we could, the methods and means of personal growth in community. Now, therefore, we may have to go back to the lessons we should have learned in our childhood. Once there was a time when

31

we liked things because we liked them, with no inward or outward pressure to justify those spontaneous preferences. We were quite simply ourselves—not very good selves, probably, but not trying to be or appear to be other than ourselves. We cannot unmake our adult identities. We cannot jettison our history. We cannot go back to the childish simplicities. But we can reclaim ourselves, and to become spiritual, we must. For us, as "for the hermit, the best sign that he is unified within himself is the reconciliation, in him, of all the ages of life".[1]

How? Primarily by recovering the child's honesty in receiving experience while retaining the adult's understanding of our involvement with other people and things. By acting from within our own selves yet adapting those actions to the situations we happen to be in. By combining the courage of the young with the courtesy of the mature. By admitting the confusions within us and the complexities around us without abandoning in despair the search for a flexible and creative order. By accepting ourselves as the persons we veritably are.

"Take what you want, says God, and pay for it"— so runs a Spanish proverb, and life confirms it. We choose what we shall take, and sooner or later, in one way or another, we pay the price: one price, in one coinage, for becoming persons; a different price and perhaps a different coinage for disowning ourselves. We pay one price for embarking on the way of the spirit, and a different price for embarking on other ways. No person can choose, or pay the whole price, for another, yet all of us participate at least indirectly in all choices, facilitating or hindering them, and each of us is wounded or healed by every choice of a way of life, his own and all others.

∙ ∙ ∙

Much has been said and written, in many spiritual traditions, about the need to lose ourselves, to give ourselves away, to become nothing so that, being empty, we can be filled with the spirit, the light, the ultimate, or however we name it. Before we can negate our selves, however, we must *be* selves. A nonentity cannot relate itself to the ultimate, the unreal to the supremely real. We cannot lose, give up, empty out what we do not have. During our novitiate, therefore, self-fulfillment in our loves, our work, our recreating recreations, does not constitute deviation from the spiritual life. It is essential.

Our nothingness before the ultimate is one thing. Nothingness within ourselves is something else. In some traditions it is taken for granted that everyone is by nature selfish, self-willed, suffused with pride, and blind to his own sins and aberrations. That does indeed obtain in some cases, and for those people, disciplines such as daily examinations of conscience and frequent acts of contrition can be invaluable correctives. Also common, however, are persons of another kind, often—very often—found in the West among women, Blacks, ethnics, and homosexuals (among others), and more blatantly among the Untouchables of India, the Eta of Japan, and other outcasts in other cultures. Not all members of those groups are afflicted with an acute sense of their intrinsic unworthiness, but for the many who are, constant rehearsals of their misdeeds can lead to states that are spiritually as well as psychologically diseased.

Augustine of Hippo reports God as saying, "I am the food of the full-grown; become a man and thou shalt feed on Me".[2] And the author of the Epistle to the Hebrews writes, "Strong meat belongeth to them that are of full age, even those who by reason of use have their senses exercised to discern both good and evil".[3] To grow into our fullness means not denying our capacities and abilities, our knowledge and values, our traits, attitudes, interests, and styles, or our place in the world. Neither does it mean refusing to develop and enjoy them. "Humility does not consist in thinking yourself a worm," Charles Williams wrote,[4] or in trying to become one. Rather, it consists in being as complete as we can be in order to give the more. A meager self is a meager gift to the ultimate. At the other extreme, arrogance does not give at all.

From beginning to end, the life of the spirit is empowered and channeled by three conditions. We are social beings. We are individual persons. And we belong in the world as part of it, acting, observing, and evaluating.

We were conceived by an act that is social in its nature and consequences, a relation between two people who—however ignorant or uncaring, and however brief their alliance—were yet socially related. We were born into a society, even though in an extreme instance it might have consisted of only two members, the mother and her child. Without attention from someone else, we would have died soon after birth of starvation or exposure. Our advent evoked a response from society, which since our birth has had to determine and continually re-determine how it will behave toward us: whether to nurture or neglect us, and in what manner, according to what procedures. Our languages of word and action, our concepts of rights and duties, our understanding of the world and ourselves,

34

all reflect the constraints as well as the opportunities our societies have provided for us. No detail of our lives will ever be wholly free from the impact of other people or their lives from the impact of ours. Even if we isolate ourselves, our withdrawal itself has an influence, and what we did and left undone before our isolation have their effects on others.

We are also individual persons, distinguished by our characteristic traits, attitudes, interests, and styles, our abilities, knowledge, and values, our capacities and embodiments and states. Even identical twins do not have identical fingerprints or thoughts. No two of us have quite the same physical equipment or physiological equilibrium, much less the same mental capacities to receive, respond to, and interpret our experience. And we are not only different from one another; in some sense we are separate from every other. When my finger is cut, yours does not bleed. The dinner you eat does not satisfy my hunger. We can never walk exactly in another's footsteps or see through his eyes. Our bodies as well as our personal characteristics divide us individually at the same time that they supply the means and necessity for our social union.

Philosophers have debated for centuries whether the world of which we are a part—the world of earth, persons, buildings, machines, sky, animals—is real or an illusion of our unenlightened minds. For our purposes, those arguments are less important than the observation (which all of the major disputants agree upon) that the world appears to be outside us: sharply so in some cases, in others less distinctly. An African priest can lay his hand on a tree and feel the unity of its sap with his blood. A Hindu may be able to identify

35

himself with the life of an insect or a stone. Few West-
erners can discern such oneness even with another
human being. Yet always some distinction is made.
The tree, the insect, the stone, the other person, are
never "myself" in quite the same way that I am myself. In some sense or degree, the other has a life
independent of mine and hidden from me, as mine
is independent of and hidden from him. The mountains do not perish when I cease to look at them or
when I die. If a building in a distant city is hit by a
bomb, my life is diminished, but not destroyed as it
would be if the building collapsed upon my body.

We are persuaded that the world is external to us
partly because it so steadfastly resists us by imposing
constraints upon what it is possible for us to do and
be. Whatever powers may be available to exceptional
individuals, ordinarily we do not procure food merely
by thinking about it, or build highways merely by
wishing they were there, or exchange ideas with another person except by consciously formulating our
thoughts and making some effort to understand him.
A recalcitrant world, however, is not by definition a
hostile one. While its opposition can indeed be felt
as antagonistic, it can also be felt as indifferent or as
benignly upholding us. If the chair is strong enough
to resist our weight, we can relax in it. The constancy
of friends sustains us when we are troubled. As G. K.
Chesterton writes in "A Prayer in Darkness",

> Thank God the stars are set beyond my
>   power,
>   If I must travail in a night of wrath;
>   Thank God my tears will never vex a moth,
> Nor any curse of mine cut down a flower.[5]

The person who prays is at once a social being and an individual self. Therefore, whatever else spiritual life may be, it is at least social as well as individual, and it involves a relation with an other whose otherness we recognize by its resistance to our purposes and behaviors, as well as by its support in our weaknesses and uncertainties. Moreover, because we are not accidentally but intrinsically social beings, there is a real sense in which we are not alone even in our strictest isolation. Therefore spirituality is not "what we do with our solitariness", but a way of life that involves us wholly, whether at the moment we happen to be in solitude or in company, and it involves as well the wholeness—the totality—of the world.

Spiritual awakening can occur gradually or suddenly and at any time from childhood to old age. A child or adolescent, especially, will frequently isolate the experience, in part from modesty, in part from plain ignorance of what is going on. But he is not likely to forget it. It remains as a touchstone, perhaps not consciously, but none the less a criterion by which he measures other experiences. And when in later life the sense of an absence or presence becomes compelling, he can see that original awareness as the first decisive event in his spiritual journey: the seed that had been growing all that time in the darkness of his preoccupations until he was ready to cultivate it.

CHAPTER TWO

Under the Aspect of Eternity

O world invisible, we view thee,
O world intangible, we touch thee,
O world unknowable, we know thee,
Inapprehensible, we clutch thee!

Francis Thompson
"In No Strange Land"

We are human by our genetic endowment. We become persons by interacting with others who, by treating us personally, create for us a situation in which we must respond as persons or know ourselves to be defective in meeting the demands of the occasion. As persons, we are part of a world in which we are not entirely at home, and which sometimes surprises us. Sometimes we respond to those astonishing events with wondering awe. A story, a landscape, a birth or death, an example of courage or love, a question or answer, a violation or aberration, lays a stillness upon us. The moment comes of its own accord, or does not come. The music lover may attend many concerts, the nature lover walk many trails, with delight but not the unmistakable invasion of rapture. The veteran nurse or soldier may apparently be hardened against every horror, yet suddenly be pierced by a majestic dread. Time and again over the years we are burdened by guilt without being tormented by any sense of sin.

Wonder is the taproot of worship, but whether the tree grows to maturity, and flowers and bears fruit, depends upon our nurturing it, or at the very least upon our not stunting it or cutting it down. Nothing compels us to follow that leading away from the mundane, but also, nothing can prevent us from doing so.

One of the simplest occasions for wonder is natural admiration: we encounter something that is greater than ourselves in some way or ways. Individually we are less comprehensive than the world, less enduring in time than humanity, less powerful than earthquakes and tornadoes, less intelligent, wise, competent, good, than many other persons we encounter daily. Whatever or whomever we acknowledge to be greater than we are—death or disease, a moral principle or an intellectual discipline, an anthropomorphic deity or an anthropic hero—most of us admit more or less willingly the existence of some greater-than-ourselves which commands our admiration.

Beyond admiration lies wonder, and beyond wonder, worship, which in the sense I am using the word means more than a high degree of admiration. Admiring, we lift up our eyes. Worshipping, we fall to our knees. Figuratively or literally we abase ourselves—quite possibly standing with our arms and eyes raised in adoration. Admiration and adoration are compatible, although they are not necessarily conjoined. People have worshipped although they feared the object of their worship, and without in any way liking or approving of its nature and power, simply because they believed it to be supremely powerful.

Do we first worship some perceptible or definable thing or person, or do we start with the awareness of a general "other" and later come to know it more specifically? I suspect that the sequence is not the same for everyone, and I am not prepared to assert the intrinsic superiority of either approach over the other. But in a time when worship itself is so often derided, and prayer has become an empty word, the question, "Can I worship at all?" must take precedence over "What can I worship?"

The one element in personal life which absolutely precludes worship is hardness of heart. We can be compelled by bodily or psychological pressures to bend our knees; we cannot be compelled to bow our hearts. If we spend our lives looking contemptuously down ... if we steadfastly believe that we are wholly in control of our own lives ... if we are convinced that human beings are the measure of all things ... if we insist on proof that something deserves our worship before we will kneel ... we shall have taken a posture that is utterly inconsistent with kneeling or with lifting our hearts.

When our rein upon ourselves is so tight that we will not love until we have indubitable evidence that another person fully merits our love, we shall be safe against its invasion—at least until we have so blinded ourselves, in our search for the perfect beloved, that we can no longer distinguish reality from dream. Likewise, if we insist that the existence of a god or the nature of an ultimate reality be philosophically demonstrated before we will worship anything, we will harden our hearts against forms of appreciation other than the philosophical.

For many of us today, a significant barrier to worship is not that we believe it to be unreal, but that we know it is undignified. Man the Master of His Fate, Man the Crowning Achievement of Nature, renounces his position and humiliates himself by admitting that his desires and values are not the ultimate standards by which the whole world is to be judged ... that there are some things that human beings cannot do even in concert ... that the possession of power does not automatically convey the rightful authority to wield it or the ability to wield it wisely ... that confronting the ultimate, we are as children. We may accept these as doctrines without hesitation. Then instantly we turn to reconstructing the balance of nature because we are annoyed by mosquitoes, to demanding laws for the punishment of behavior not because it is wrong but because it offends our delicate tastes, to expecting that persons can be changed from hostility to friendliness by argument, and from foolishness to wisdom by more efficient methods of instruction in our schools. Carefully affirming our humility, we act as if our judgements were sure.

A purely verbal humility counts for nothing. What matters is the actions that reveal the beliefs by which we live. We do not kneel to what we believe we can control, so that as long as we maintain our self-possession in disasters and ecstasies and other events that test our equilibrium, we shall not be disposed to worship. Morever, a feeling of humility is not sufficient, which is why I speak of kneeling rather than adoring. To kneel is by definition an act, a behavior. If by legitimate extension it refers also to a mental or spiritual posture, a trait or attitude, the weight of the word is still upon deliberation and enactment.

We kneel, if at all, because (in Charles Morgan's words) we see ourselves "in a second place absolutely, and to kneel is an inward necessity".[1] For a moment or a lifetime, we acknowledge ourselves to be secondary to an ultimate. That ultimate can be apprehended through a person, a work of art, a place, a religious doctrine or ceremony—almost anything— because these are only means. We sense, beyond them, a being or state or condition that is invulnerable to the changes that beset us, and is all-encompassing. It invades us. Or we enter it. Temporarily and partially, or wholly and enduringly, we partake of its nature. And not only we as individuals: union with the ultimate encompasses us as members of communities and as participants in the world, all enclosed within the ultimate as the sky encloses our planet. We know, of course, that the sky is not a boundary, a thing, but our manner of perceiving space. Likewise we know that the ultimate which embraces space and time is not confined to our conceptions of a deity or "heaven", but to our manner of affirming that we know ourselves, and all that is, to be "in a second place absolutely". They and we exist *sub specie aeternitatis*—under the aspect of eternity.

In the experience of wonder, we touch the ultimate ... or it touches us. Worshipping, we kneel in the presence of the ultimate, giving ourselves up to that which is infinitely greater than we are, and greater than the entire mundane world. If we ask, "What is it? What do words like 'ultimate' and 'transcendent' refer to?", we move from worship to investigation, from our knees to our feet, an action that will become appropriate in its own time and will be discussed at length later on. At the stage we are now considering, the point is precisely that we do not know what it is, and we do not need to know. The finite cannot grasp the infinite. Ultimacy contains time but time cannot contain the ultimate. We can sense the absolute quality of the ultimate, although we cannot define its nature, or locate it by the coordinates of space and time. On the contrary, the ultimate lies both beyond and within all times and places, and times and places must be defined in its terms, not the other way around.

"Behind ... beyond ... before ... within ... above ...": our languages compel us to speak of the transcendent ultimate as if it had a place in the world, or as if it were an entity or a being. No human language can entirely free us from our human condition as finite creatures in space and time, so that the remedy for our incapacity is not to keep silent, but rather to concede that here is one of the situations where we must speak figuratively—and should be courteous both in choosing our figures of speech and in interpreting those which others are using. Does anyone cavil at the phrase ,"an idea in the back of my mind", although it is nonsense if taken literally? Ideas do not reside in places, and minds are not containers like closets. Why, then, be captious about "God in heaven", or agitate whether the ultimate is "out there" or "in here"? Whatever their form, these statements are figurative.

They express not intellectual assent but imaginative vitality. They do not persuade the mind, but impregnate it.

To speak of the ultimate as the absolute and final other, overarching and permeating all that is, commits us only to the position that we are in a second place absolutely. We have fallen to our knees, not losing ourselves in a perpetual haze of emotionalism but taking the ultimate as our point or frame of reference for all our experience. So doing, we accept ungrudgingly that we are not the center of the universe. Worship permits, but does not require, that we postulate a deity. It does require that we know ourselves in relation to something qualitatively different from and transcending ourselves, and so much higher or greater or deeper than we are that spontaneously we abase ourselves before it.

Those of us who use pictorial images or intellectual models in our thinking will probably adopt ancient symbols for the ultimate, or construct new ones, as an aid in focussing our devotional activities. But we are not restricted to a single image or model. Two or ten or a constellation may serve us better than a single one. An image is something we look through in order to discern a more profound or significant reality. It is like the lenses of a telescope or microscope. But one image alone, such as that of light or power or a person, tends to degenerate into an idol—something we look at for its own sake—more readily than a combination of images that correct and supplement each other: a God-man, a compelling light, a personal power, a Father/Mother.

Setting aside the threat of idolatry, it may not matter

much whether we begin to worship with or without images, by praising or petitioning or confessing our guilt, in public or in private. Indeed, it may be a mistake to begin our experiments in worship by trying doggedly to praise or petition or to feel a sense of emptiness or sin. We may be already too self-conscious about worshipping, too niggling in our approach to the most high, however we conceive of it or her or him or them. Possibly we should abandon our theories and established practices, and neither attempt to pray nor resist our spontaneous impulses toward worship, but wait for them to happen.

And they will, because prayer and worship are as natural as loving, admiring, desiring, and feeling shame. These functions may not appear natural. We have stultified our loves with intellectual theories, our admirations with schools of criticism, our guilts with psychological interpretations, and our devotional tendencies with inappropriate disciplines, until they have become poor, feeble things. Our religious instruction may have given us the impression that worship is an art to be learned like operatic singing, rather than a natural function like breathing. We have taken great pains, therefore, to master advanced techniques—exact pitch, precise enunciation, subtle phrasing—but have done nothing to improve the column of air which is molded by the throat and mouth. "Learning to worship", like "learning to breathe properly", is not an achievement of a new power, but the discipline and refinement of a basically natural and ordinary activity.

It is tempting to diagnose such errors as a consequence of thinking too much. More frequently, they follow from thinking in the wrong way: rationally rather than personally, that is, with the celibate intellect rather than a connubial union of analytical with imaginative ways of thinking. Temporarily, therefore, it may be good for us to stop thinking about what worship is, and how and when to pray, stilling the impatient, probing mind until it has something worth probing: a perception, a response, an experience that is more substantial than an abstract concept or theory. Such intellectual operations as analysis, comparison, evaluation, and system-building may be requisites for a perfected devotional life (authorities differ on this), but at certain stages in its development they are irrelevant, and can be destructive. If we approach a painting with the primary intention of appraising its merits, we shall not be receptive to it. Our network of critical principles will warp our vision. As C. S. Lewis points out, "You cannot be armed to the teeth and surrendered at the same moment".[2]

If our rudimentary stirrings toward prayer and worship are met with a barrage of questions ("Is this what the mystics are talking about?" "Am I being naïve or gullible?" "What has generated this effect?"), our ability to wonder will be diminished. Only after we have surrendered in awe, and have allowed the experience to develop, can we dissect it critically with reasonable assurance of preserving its essential qualities and its power.

I do not know of any rule for determining the point at which the intellect can productively enter the process except to follow one's intuition, and intuition is a notoriously unreliable guide. Yet intuition, like any other ability, can be trained, or, more precisely, we can be trained in its use.

To forestall possible misunderstanding, by "intuition" I do not mean some special, mysterious ability akin, perhaps, to the psychic. Rather, I mean what we know without being able to offer any evidence for it. Thus ordinary observation is intuitive, as in "It's dark in here". So also are "I remember what happened" and "I've just realized that those ideas are related". An intuition is an immediate apprehension, a starting-point. It is not, however, foolproof. Our observation may be mistaken, our memory at fault, our realization in error, but we have ways to check them out: among other ways, by acting on them and seeing what happens—accumulating evidence, if you will, to confirm or disconfirm our intuitive knowledge.

We can have immediate apprehensions—intuitions—of a situation, a relationship, a work of art, a book, summarizing what they are. Such intuitive summaries can be on any scale: a single book or an author's lifelong production; a football game, or a particular play, or an individual player's performance, or a football season as a whole.

One of the marks of an expert in any field—a football coach, for instance—consists in his ability to see at a glance what is going on. An art lover immediately apprehends that this work of art is a Jacob Epstein sculpture; and how does he know? "It just looks like his work." A psychotherapist develops a "nose" for the structure of an unruly relationship, a philosopher for an elegant argument, an experienced cook for a recipe. We acquire these summarizing skills in the same way that we acquire social, manual, and other skills: by participating in social practices that involve our using them.

Learning to apprehend something or everything

under the aspect of eternity is like learning to see something or everything with an artist's or scientist's or historian's or housewife's eye. It means adopting a perspective, a viewpoint from which we observe and appraise the world, and it takes practice and experience to become adept in viewing things that way. At all levels, more often than not, implicit in that apprehension will be a course of action as, in the medical model, a diagnosis frequently implies a therapy. In such cases, often we speak of an intuition as "prompting" or "guiding" us—phrases which make it sound as if intuition were a special power rather than a summary with implications for our behavior.

Historically, the study of the disciplines and potentialities of intuition has been even more neglected than the study of the training and uses of imagination. Any hypothesis concerning what goes on in intuitive observations and summaries must therefore be offered diffidently and received circumspectly. My own conjecture is that the ultimate, of which we have only an intuitive grasp, is not passive, but that like the "force" of gravitation or the "power" of a charismatic personality, it acts upon us, not displaying itself but inciting us to move toward a consummation which we cannot discern. Yet as we yield to its pressure, we become increasingly sensitive to its motions and accurate in interpreting them, as—for example—in determining when we should exercise our analytical mind and when we should silence it.

On this hypothesis, the ultimate is not impotent or mute. It declares itself to us at its own times and in its own ways, and we can hear it if we listen without prejudice, cynicism, or fear. A decision in advance to hear only one sort of word from or about the ultimate (for example, impersonal but not personal, or vice versa), or a prior exclusion of all but one way of hearing its voice (ears, mind, intuition, imagination, or any other) does not silence it, but insulates us in a sound-proof room where no communication reaches us except the noise of our own breathing and the beating of our own hearts. When we make demands upon the ultimate, we are implicitly raising ourselves to its level or lowering it to ours. Either way, we rise from our knees and so break our lines of intercourse with whatever lies beyond the mundane.

"The gods offer their own nature to all of us", says a character in Charles Morgan's *Sparkenbroke*, "but only a god knows how to accept".[3] We are not gods; we cannot accept the nature of "the gods" in godlike measure. We can, however, submit to their impregnation, and in receiving the little that we can contain at first, we become enlarged so that we can receive more. But we cannot force the process or choose the manner of its unfolding, much less control its timing. Often, I believe, we apprehend the ultimate intuitively before we begin to worship. But the "right" sequence of events depends always upon the action of the ultimate upon the particular individual, and his particular response to it, neither of which we can determine or regulate.

In the beginning, we had better take our intuitive leadings with a grain of skepticism and two grains of practical caution. Their promptings should not be taken as infallible, and we should not allow them to lead us into situations that we cannot escape if our understanding of their counsels proves to be unproductive or ushers us into trouble. Although learning does not automatically result from doing, we can indeed learn by doing if we treat our intuitions as guides for experiments. Has our intellectual quibbling killed a budding plant? Next time we shall be more patient with those tender shoots. Have we leaped headlong into an unrewarding pursuit? Next time we shall not commit ourselves so precipitously. Thus an error does not become a disaster; even a grave blunder does not produce despair; and the identification of a dead end becomes a substantial achievement.

Adopting an experimental frame of mind does not mean "making experiments" with our worship, as by formulating hypotheses and testing them under controlled conditions, varying those conditions systematically in order to see what will happen. Prayer is not a science, and we are not—in this connection—scientists. Moreover, we do not know whether what we are looking for is an idea, a person, an experience, a transformation, or something else. Therefore we do not know what kind of experiments would be suitable for answering our questions.

But our difficulty is only half defined by saying that we do not have precise methods for answering our questions. Frequently we have only the haziest notion of what our questions are. All we are sure of is that we are haunted by an uneasiness that occasionally and briefly is relieved, or by a rare and fleeting perception of a glory that we cannot lay hold of. Because no two persons will be haunted in quite the same way, or will think of their haunting in quite the same terms, each must determine what is appropriate for his own search. For this determination by and large the most effective tool is observation. At the outset we can search without searching. We watch, we listen, we wait.

What do we wait for? The intuitive inward signal,

"Look here. Try this. Leave that alone. Go back"—
often given with no explanations, as unreasonble and
unmistakable as our reactions to tastes and smells.
Then, unless we have cogent reasons for disobeying,
we follow that inner directive. In other words, we
deliberately—though cautiously—play our hunches.

Since the value of intuitions is likely to be erratic,
it is usually advisable to check our intuitions before
we yield to them, especially when they involve other
persons. The impulse to transmit bad news or to utter
a criticism may exhibit the desire to hurt rather than
a correct perception that the other person needs the
information from us, or at all. The urgent sense that
we should refrain from a particular action may issue
from our irresponsibility or cowardice rather than from
the ultimate. Neither good intentions nor sound reasoning will save us from all such mistakes, although
the combination of good will and intelligent foresight
will avert the worst of them.

The surest guard against confusing emotional impulse with intuition is the humility which stems from
our awareness of living under an ultimate that per-
vades our intuitions. Impulse says, "This is what I
want." Intuition says. "This is what the situation calls
for"—which may or may not be what I want. Both
speak as if from within, and with authoritative voices.
Neither can be rationally justified or explained, or
tested except by its compatibility with the ultimate:
is the prompting in accord with that which evokes our
adoration? We are dealing here not with moral or intellectual issues, but with our aesthetic sense of the
fitness of things, of how things fit together in a pattern
that we have not established, but to which we and
other persons alike are subordinated.

An inclination that is contrary to emotion ("I don't

want to, but I should"), or is offensive to reason ("This sounds stupid but somehow right"), or is independent of either, presumably has some source other than emotional desires or intellectual judgements. We can tentatively exclude emotion and reason, however, without positively identifying the source of the promptings. We know very little of these matters; there may well be more involved than what I have mentioned so far: emotion, intellect, and intuition.

Limiting ourselves for the time being to those three, however, we must note that any of them may impel us toward either fulfilment or destruction, either joy or despair, either glory or outrage. Granting for the moment that some of our intuitions reflect our relation with an ultimate, we must watch whether our response to the ultimate is—in words taken from an ancient tradition—godlike or devilish. At the very beginning, we may not be able to differentiate a will-o'-the-wisp from the divine pillar of fire, so that most of our learning will be by trial and error, with many errors ranging from dire to hilarious—and with now and again a stunningly successful trial.

Learning and maturation in the life of the spirit cannot be hurried, and as in physical and intellectual development, a great deal depends upon our readiness. Children cannot learn to walk or to read before their muscular, nervous, and other systems are ready; neither can we become competent in—let us say—contemplation or intercessory prayer before we are ready. Here again our most reliable guide will be intuition, backed by such information as we can acquire on different kinds of prayer.

Some of the theoretical possibilities will be eliminated by our circumstances. Trying out the meditative practices of yoga or T'ai Chi is hardly practicable if there is no teacher of that discipline available, and saying the rosary will not appeal to someone not of a Roman Catholic background. A person who sits at a desk or bench for forty hours a week may well find that walking meditation, as in Zen practice, is more conducive to worship than prolonged kneeling. One whose work requires intense intellectual effort and concentration may find that improvisational dance, or emptying the mind in "the prayer of centering", is more worshipful than a spiritual discipline which requires periods of close mental attention. Conversely, a mother with small children, who is interminably being pulled this way and that, may soar spiritually under a discipline that calls her to focus her thoughts, even though briefly and intermittently.

Because spirituality is not separable from the person in his situation, the form that our spirituality takes will be unduly restricted and restrictive unless it takes into account all our personal characteristics and all our circumstances. A gentle waiting upon the Lord may be the most productive form of spirituality for a compuslive perfectionist, but the chances are that it will be wrong for the lazy or the capricious. Those who live under persecution are called to forms of spirituality different from those available to persons who are living in a supportive community. No form is intrinsically higher or lower than any other, but there are marked differences one from another, as we can see vividly when we look at the lives of "saints" in various traditions. In Christianity, for example, they range from warriors (Joan of Arc) to peacemakers (Francis of Assisi), from scholars (Thomas Aquinas) to the illiterate (Julian of Norwich), and from members of cloistered orders (John of the Cross) to men and women who are politically influential in the world (Philip Neri, Catherine of Siena).

The remarkable diversity of the saints, at least in the Christian tradition, is unmistakable evidence of the diversity of spiritual ways. And a maxim of Søren Kierkegaard's suggests how we can discover which way is *our* way: "By relating oneself to oneself, and by willing to be oneself, one is grounded transparently in the power that constituted the self".[4] As long as we pretend to ourselves that we are other than we are, or try to become what is incompatible with what we are, we cannot be "grounded transparently in the power" that has made us what we are. The legend of St Christopher, physically a giant, tells that his spiritual mentor ordered him to fast and pray, but he refused to fast on the ground that fasting would deprive him of the strength that was his primary means for serving God. And by his refusal to be other than himself, the way opened for him to be uniquely a Christ-bearer.

Willing to be oneself is not always easy, especially when in the first place we are not at all sure who we are, and in the second, we repudiate fervently certain aspects of ourselves: our hasty temper, our dependency, our talkativeness, our untidiness. We can say, perhaps, that what we really are is the self which is trying to be more even-tempered, independent, taciturn, neat, but this can lead us into trouble. Our self-selected self may be a lion attempting to be a lamb, or a sparrow to be a whale. Perhaps, instead of straining to curb our anger, we should redirect it against brutality and injustice. Perhaps, we are dependent by nature or our present circumstances make us so, and we should accept our dependence and even rejoice in it.

As far as I know, the only way to find out who we are is indirectly, by living as we already do until we can no longer live that way, and then—in Charles Morgan's image—go on a voyage into another way of life, as naturally as a migratory bird takes off in autumn and spring.[5] Not all of us have the bird's built-in sense for when it is time to migrate, or its accuracy in finding its proper destination. We may have to go on a number of voyages—try out several ways of life—before we end, each leading into the next. And whether the succession of voyages continues after our death, nobody knows, although many are sure. In this life, however, some keep to one way of life straightforwardly from start to finish; others embrace one for almost a lifetime before they move on; still others, in their voyages, dart from one port to another before they come home.

"I *am* the person who lives *this* way of life, and therefore has *this* place in the world". To an important degree, the communities within which we live prescribe our place, but ultimately, we prescribe our own. We can accept the place they assign to us, or we can ignore or defy it. If we accept, is it from conviction or cowardice? If we ignore or defy, is it in obedience to a higher authority or in arrogance? There are no guarantees. All we can do is to live the way in which, under the aspect of eternity, we are called to live, to see if we *can* live that way.

This approach can be described as "doing what comes naturally", but only in the sense of its being compatible with our intrinsic nature as human beings and as individual persons. Some traditions teach that for the fulfilment of our deepest or highest natures, we must repudiate such "natural" desires as for worldly security, comfort, self-esteem, self-direction, and so on. So they impose observances designed to curb our "lower" natures, for example by celibacy, restricted diets, interrupted sleep, rough clothing, and harsh penalties for infractions even in thought. In some cases, this ascetic spirituality reflects the view that human nature is inherently either evil or earthbound, or both, and must be forcibly detached from its sinful or mundane heritage before it can come into the presence of the ultimate. In other words—according to this thesis–unless we do violence to our natural selves, we cannot rise above our old selves so as to live under the aspect of eternity.

This is not my way, so I cannot write of it from inner knowledge, or indeed with much sympathy, partly because I do not agree with that assessment of human nature. There are, however, ways of life that look very much like those forcible repudiations but are derived from another root, another doctrine of human nature. Some people deliberately choose poverty, celibacy, and other forms of what most of us would call severe deprivations, as enabling a way of life which they prefer to other ways—as others might prefer mountain climbing to watching television or playing the piano to shopping for new clothes. From the outside, the acceptance of poverty, celibacy, and so on may look like monstrous sacrifices. From the inside, they can be merely a stripping away of non-essentials, as welcome as undressing before a swim on a hot day. G. K. Chesterton puts it succinctly: "The most formidable liberal philosophers have called the monks melancholy because they denied themselves the pleasures of liberty and marriage. They might as well call the trippers on a Bank Holiday melancholy because they deny themselves, as a rule, the pleasures of silence and meditation".[6]

Swimming, mountain-climbing, and piano-playing, if taken seriously, will be strenuous and, upon occasion, painful activities. They all require renunciations and continuing disciplines which are accepted willingly for the sake of the enterprise and the achievement. Likewise, the person who embarks on a spiritual way of life will embrace certain disciplines and renounce non-essentials, not merely "to obtain mastery over himself", but because these choices enable him to do what he wants to do and be what he wants to be. A discipline that does not serve those ends will be a waste of energy: a mountain-climber does not need to become proficient in the five-finger exercises that a concert pianist practises daily. But both must develop the ability to concentrate for long stretches of time. In neither case are they doing violence to their intrinsic natures; they are simply channeling their efforts in one direction rather than another.

I have heard the objection that if all we do is "what comes naturally", we shall never change from what and where we are. That is like saying that if all we do is follow where our curiosity leads, we shall never learn anything. The spiritual impetus, like the impetus of curiosity, can and not infrequently does result in radical personal change. Curiosity motivates explorers, scientists, scholars, and others—including children. The drive toward spirituality is no less compelling than that toward satisfying curiosity, and is no less revolutionary in its consequences.

So far, we have given a good deal of attention to the experiences of surprise, wonder, worship, but we have not looked at all at "religious experience". And we will not look at it again in these pages except in passing, for three reasons. First, the literature on spirituality is already filled to repletion with descriptions of what religious experiences feel like. Second, the experience is generally taken to be indescribable. And third, it is relatively unimportant.

"Religious experience" as such is indescribable not because it is ineffable to a degree beyond other experiences—that is arguable—but because it is always particular, like meeting a friend or crossing the street. What does it feel like to meet a friend or to cross a street? The only possible answer is, "Whatever it feels like". Those experiences are set apart not by the feelings that accompany what happens, but by the happenings themselves.

Likewise, the distinctive element in meeting the ultimate is the meeting itself, not what it feels like. Our feelings do not authenticate the event; the event authenticates whatever feelings we happen to have. If we remember this, it will save us from the pitfall of trying—or expecting—to reproduce in ourselves the experiences we read of in Julian of Norwich, Augustine of Hippo, George Fox, John Donne, and a host of others. Becoming conversant with their accounts of their experiences can be of value to us, in the same way that reading about the experience of falling in love can enlighten us about what is going on when we do fall in love. But in both cases, there is the danger that the information we acquire from others will tempt us into generating inauthentic emotions, and into testing our actual meetings by false criteria.

The correspondence between falling in love and meeting the ultimate can be carried further. We can ask of either, "Is this the real thing or a delusion, mere infatuation or mere fantasy?" Nothing in the experience *as experience* distinguishes infatuation from real love. The difference lies in what we do with the experience: in infatuation, we abandon the relationship when the initial glory fades, as it inevitably will; in love, we commit ourselves to the growth and strengthening of the relationship. Similarly, when we have what we think may be a glimpse or vision of a transcendent reality, our question should be not the speculative "Was it true?" but the practical "How shall I act on it?" It is not entirely accurate to say that it *is* what we make of it, but what we do make of it will contribute mightily to our discovering what it is. Further, of course, our making will also disclose much about who we are.

Falling in love is ecstatic and transitory, like the mystical vision, and other decisive encounters with the ultimate that are less extreme. Enduring love is less dramatic, glowing rather than dazzling, and even so, not glowing steadily. Characteristically, romantic love and spiritual living alike have intervals of conflict, dryness, and darkness, occasionally lasting for years, when the relationship endures only because we are committed to persevere in it. The initial rapture may recur upon occasion, but it is not to be compelled or sought after, and essentially its presence or absence is incidental. The experiences are not central to the nature of the relationship. And the goal in both cases is not deliverance from pain, suffering, and mental anguish, and not knowledge or power, but illumination, and the truly abundant life includes in its fullness not only consolation but also desolation, and is marked by holiness.

The person who lives under the aspect of eternity does not live there alone. We are social beings not from habit, and not for convenience or expediency, but of necessity. Human beings can be isolated; a *person* in isolation is a contradiction in terms. We are and continue to be persons because we live in community with other persons.

The manner of our community, however, is not fixed. We can be gregarious or solitary, or both by turns, and express our social nature as well by private prayer as by serving on a committee devoted to civic betterment or cooking dinner for our family. It makes no difference here which activities represent the most efficacious mode of social involvement. They are all social practices, actions expressing our interdependence with others. Thus even if we are not at the moment conscious of others' presence, their participation in us and ours in them persists, so that we carry them with us into the light of the ultimate. As our relationship with the ultimate influences all our behavior, so in some sense all persons with whom we are in relation are with us there. No matter how deep our solitude, we are not isolated unless we deliberately repudiate our social heritage and fruition, including our responsibility for the results of our withdrawal.

Further, since the ultimate *is* ultimate because it overarches all that is, the sense of its presence and activity binds us to other persons. We may be its sole worshipper, and we may not be able to define or describe or name it, but we see it as universally authoritative, as gravitational forces have power over those who have never heard of the law of gravitation, as well as upon those who know it by name.

It is possible, though by no means certain, that the highest forms of worship are those which are achieved in the midst of the turmoil of life, not apart from it, but a great many of us find it easier—especially at the beginning—to attain stillness of spirit in solitude than in company. Usually, the fully developed life of the spirit seems to require that the person enter and pass through various stages, such as solitude and social activity, before he reaches spiritual maturity. But as far as I can discover, there are no universally applicable rules which spell out where and how all persons should begin or end their journeys, or in what order they should go through the stages. For example, it seems to be desirable, if not necessary, for complete spiritual development that at some period or periods the person should believe in an anthropomorphic god or gods, and that in other periods he should abandon that notion. Many people hold that anthropomorphism is appropriate only for small children and the senile, and should be discouraged even in them. In neither the history nor the theology of the devotional life can I find any justification for such a conclusion, or for so dogmatic an attitude toward the processes of growth. On the contrary, what appear to be critical are the rhythm and timing of the movement, which depend both upon the style of the person in relation to the constancies and fluctuations of his life, and upon the ultimate itself.

We begin the life of the spirit where we are: believing or not believing in a diety; active in a congenial or uncongenial group or off by ourselves; with or without a clear and coherent world view; emotionally torn or serene; intellectually cynical or skeptical or confident or credulous. All starting places are valid that reflect the person's turning away from the mundane to an ultimate that embraces all that is, whether it is the baby's appeal to the parents who are ultimate for him, or the mystic's gratitude for the vision of ineffable glory. Once this precondition has been fulfilled, we are ready to begin the work of prayer, to learn what facilitates and what hinders our worship, and to consider a few of the multitudinous ways that the life of the spirit can be lived.

PART TWO

The Work of Prayer

Daily, though no ears attended,
Did my prayers arise.
Daily, though no fires descended,
Did I sacrifice.
Though my darkness did not lift,
Though I faced no lighter odds,
Though the Gods bestowed no gift,
None the less,
None the less, I served the Gods!

Rudyard Kipling
"The Obedient"

CHAPTER THREE

Approaching the Ultimate

God does not die on the day when we cease to believe in a personal deity, but we die on the day when our lives cease to be illumined by the steady radiance, renewed daily, of a wonder, the source of which is beyond all reason.

Dag Hammarskjöld
Markings

Our approaches to the ultimate can be grouped in terms of three basic movements. We reach out to grasp. We open ourselves. We present an offering.

Because at the beginning we know only vaguely what we are reaching for and what we are opening ourselves to, we may do best by flinging out our gestures with the abandon of a dandelion releasing its seeds into the wind, uttering praises and entreaties not specifically to a deity, but to anyone or anything that is able to receive them, or begging for help with no preconceptions about who or what will provide it, or how or even whether an answer will be given. Blinded by darkness or excessive light, we shout in the hope of hearing from somewhere—anywhere—a reply.

"Help me! Give me!" Or, "Help us! Give us!" "Heal the child ... Send us food ... Save us from our enemy ... Grant us thy peace." If only we can take hold of the creative energies that infuse the cosmos, surely they will deliver us. And apparently they do— not always, by any means, but often enough that it is commonplace to hear of instances where "the power of positive thinking", or chanting "Namu myoho renge kyo" before the gohonzon, or the petition to the saint has been followed by what seemed to be a direct answer to prayer. Did we effect that result? Have we benefited from a miracle? Is the ultimate subject to our control?

The question can better be asked in a negative form. What forces in the universe, if any, are *not* under our control? In theory, if not yet in practice, we can manipulate winds and waves, temperatures and rains. We have created living organisms in test tubes, and computers that perform many "human" functions. Extrasensory perception is demonstrated in laboratories, and religious and quasi-scientific groups without number have collected testimony that we can change events, persons, and things by concentrating and projecting our thoughts without any known physical intermediary. From fire-walking to communicating with the dead, and from witchcraft to faith-

66

healing, examples abound of what some call fraud or delusion, and others call answers to prayer.

Where do we draw the lines between control by scientific methods, by some kind of mental or psychic force, and by prayer? I do not think we can with any precision, and I do not believe that here it is necessary even to try. Functionally and from the human point of view (which is the only point of view we have), all three ways are the same in one crucially important respect: *we* are taking the initiative. The techniques are different, but what is going on is our attempt to direct what happens, applying whatever energies we can muster toward curing the disease, quieting the conflict, correcting the error, or freeing the sinner from his sin or the obsessed from his obsession.

To ask whether such "natural" prayers, whether for good or evil ends, are legitimate or effective is like asking whether curiosity is legitimate and effective. The petitions come as naturally to us as the questions "Why?" and "How?" They can be blocked, as curiosity also can be ("You're not supposed to ask—or ask for—that"), and like curiosity, they can be misguided. Invasions of privacy, for instance, either by peering through our neighbor's window or by manipulating his behavior without his knowledge or consent, are in bad taste if not morally wrong. Intrinsically, such "natural" prayers are like other natural powers: neither good nor evil in themselves, but only as we use them for good or evil ends.

In principle, we should be able to determine whether these "natural" prayers are effective, what proportion are answered favorably, unfavorably, or apparently are unanswered, and under what conditions each occurs. The difficulties in obtaining significant results would be formidable, but the study might tell us a good deal about what persons are capable of. And it might perhaps teach us something about the far and deep reaches of the natural universe where scientists have not yet explored. Thus a careful investigation of intercessory prayer as portrayed in Charles Williams' *Descent into Hell* could conceivably change our scientific and philosophical concepts of time, with startling practical consequences. Or we might become able to move mountains with no implements other than our faith. But as Charles Morgan writes,

> Miracles are not an arbitrary magic but a summoning of those reserves of nature which underlie common experience. They are more natural than what we call nature; that is what is exceptional about them—they are *more* natural, not less. . . . The skeptical and credulous . . . in certain ways they are very alike. It's as if they were living in an enclosed harbour and had forgotten the sea outside. One day the sea flows in strongly; there is an exceptional tide; and one says that it's impossible, that it isn't true, and the other throws up her hands and says it's a stroke of magic. Both forget the sea outside and that it is always there and always connected with the water in the harbour. . . .[1]

They forget, too, that dikes can be built to prevent the sea from flowing into the harbor or, conversely, pumps installed to draw the water into landlocked regions.

•   •   •

Natural prayers are not to be scorned because they appear selfish or childish, or attempts to shape events to our desires. The movement to seize and use the fundamental energies of the universe is one way of approaching the ultimate, and if that is where we are ready to begin, we should begin there. Special danger lies at two points, however. The first is making any prayer a test case. "God, if you protect me on this journey, I shall know you love me. If I have an accident, I will conclude that you hate me or are indifferent to me, or that you do not exist at all." From such evidence as we have, the ultimate simply does not submit so passively to our demands for proof, or give such clear-cut answers. In some traditions, it is forbidden: "Thou shalt not tempt the Lord thy God",[2]—that is, put him to the test. Our safe return demonstrates nothing about the ultimate. Nor does our suffering a major accident or death. Either may have been the result of innumerable other factors permitted, though not necessarily willed, by a deity, or governed by the laws of cause and effect, or whatever it is that orders the universe. If proof is what we want, we shall not get it by this method, and in any case, it is quite possible that proof, in its full meaning, is not attainable by finite beings in any ultimate matter. We may have excellent reasons for believing that all prayers *are* answered. In good intellectual conscience, however, the most we can say is what the scientist says about gravitation: given the data we now have, *this* way of fitting them together makes the most sense. And we may not want to say that much.

A second danger is that we may begin to feel ourselves equal with the ultimate—as if when we ask, we can depend upon its granting our wish as we depend upon a close friend to do us a favor. It makes little or no difference whether we reduce the distance between us and the ultimate by lifting ourselves up or by bringing the ultimate down to our level: either way, the creative tension slackens, like a rubber band stretched between two fingers when one of them slips out of the loop. The fingers had been connected while the rubber band held them, and the farther apart the hands, the more energy ran from one to the other. But if one hand releases the rubber band, the two hands are no longer joined. So if we diminish the "otherness" of an "other", we are connected loosely, not powerfully and firmly. An ultimate that is within our grasp, a power that we can manipulate and exploit, cannot draw us out of ourselves or impregnate us with transcendence.

Rightly used, natural prayer is a request, a declaration, an outpouring, rather than a demand or an effort to compel what is beyond us. And what we receive is a reply, not compliance with our directive. Fundamentally, however, natural prayers are a form of self-assertion, which may be a preparation for confronting the ultimate, or a desirable preliminary, or a valid accompaniment. Or they may be superfluous or—if abused—an obstruction. But the movement we make in these natural prayers is not the same as the wonder which prepares us for worship. Confronting the ultimate, we do not assert ourselves or our desires; instead, we declare the primacy of that ultimate. We do not seek; we submit to being found. Above all, before the ultimate—*sub specie aeternitatis*—we do not know; we are known.

• • •

One of the most elemental prayers to the ultimate is simply, "Thou art there. I am here." It need not be delivered in those words or in any words: we are dealing with a relationship, not a proposition, although analyzing the words may help to clarify what is going on.

Why do some of us persist in saying "Thou art" rather than "You are" or "It is"? It is because we are being touched, known, invaded in the central depth from which we respond and act most intimately. That depth has only one voice, the personal one. When we detach ourselves from the encounter by saying, "It is", we are implicitly denying that we are meeting and being met *personally*. Note that we are not using these pronouns as philosophical definitions of the ultimate or of persons, but instead as descriptions of the terms on which we meet that ultimate. The meeting itself is not the time or place for the imposition of logical categories or impersonal language upon our experience, although the logical and impersonal are appropriate for our later thinking and perhaps talking about the meeting.

Traditionally many people have chosen to say "Thou" instead of "You" when they address the ultimate in English and certain other languages, because "thou", "thee", and "thy"—the second person singular—are more formal and more intimate than "you" and "your"—the second person plural. For the exalted occasion, naturally we rise—if we can—to exalted language. Or if our image of meeting the ultimate is one of inwardness, we seek an extraordinarily intimate mode of speech for so interior an occasion. Similarly, in our goings and comings among our fellows, at times we want to address them by formal titles and at other times by pet names, because only with such words can we express the special quality of our relationship to them.

Again we are not making a metaphysical commitment at this point, which is one of the reasons why I have been using the comparatively neutral term "ultimate" in referring to it/her/him/them, rather than words like God or the gods, or the Ground of Being, or Power or Life. The "thou" defines the level of our response not the nature of the ultimate. We can, however, and we do decide how we shall imagine it: as impersonal law or a personal deity, as many or one. In speaking of or to the ultimate, sometimes we are clear whether we are using words figuratively or literally; at other times we are not. Are Kali and Apollo and Yahweh supposed to personify abstract principles, or to be persons? Do we refer impersonally to "Life" or "the Tao" from conviction or indecision, or for convenience?

Sometimes it is well not to define too closely the manner in which we use our language, either with others or in the privacy of our thoughts. We may not be ready to commit ourselves, even while we are on our knees, to any concept more definite than the Most High or the Most Profound, the End or the Beginning, or simply the Ultimate or the Transcendent. On the other hand, we may have gone in a direction other than those of logical concepts and imaginative symbols, into sheer negation. "The readiness is all", and only experimentation can tell us what we are ready for. Neither for ourselves nor for others can we assert, as a general rule, that figurative language is more appropriate than abstractions, or less appropriate, any more than we can assert that in general, worship by means of images is superior or inferior to worship without them. The supreme form of worship for one person may be the mystical vision, for another the familiar serenity of the daily Eucharist, for a third the back-breaking, heart-breaking labor to correct social evils, for a fourth the sacrificial offering of all his possessions, for a fifth, the entry into nothingness.

One of the principal functions of experimentation in the life of the spirit is to determine which of these modes of worship, or of uncounted others, most effectively enhances our awareness of the ultimate, and facilitates our surrender to it. And the need to experiment is never outgrown. Our situation changes. We change. To our astonishment if not our dismay, the figure of a person imposes itself upon our ascetically image-less worship. Or the anthropomorphic presentation no longer casts its spell upon us and we tremble lest we are "losing our religion".

We must expect such alterations in our style, as artists take for granted not only that their work will go through a succession of styles, but also that some will find (or choose) their métier early in life and others late. Among artists, it is not considered meritorious to move from a blue period through a rose period to analytic cubism merely because Picasso did, yet among worshippers it is often supposed that there is something wrong if a person grows dissatisfied with communal prayer and stops going to church, or after years of praying without words is inwardly impelled to a form of worship in which words are essential. In the creative arts, no virtue is attached to imitating another's style, but all too often religious guides attempt to produce detailed copies of this saint or that teacher, imposing the pattern upon themselves and requiring it of others.

It can be objected that the analogy is misleading, because worship is not an art. True, but like the arts it is an activity of persons, not just of intellects, emotions, and bodies, and if in either art or worship we violate the nature of persons, what results will be without integrity or power. In our day, individuality appears to be more respected among artists than among the religious; therefore we can hope to learn from them.

Both in the West and in the East, the stereotype of "great art" is less rigid than the stereotype of "the religious life". Wide variations in style are acceptable in the one discipline and decried in the other—and I speak not about styles of behavior in the two communities of artists and the religious, but about the general agreement among artists that, for example, both representational and non-representational art can be "great", as contrasted with the general insistence of religious guides that only the militant, or only the contemplative, or only the orthodox believer, or only the activist is on the path to holiness. We see teachers of art whose own work is of one style encouraging their students to develop another style, but rarely do we hear of a quietist who emboldens an activist in religion, or a rebel against a religious orthodoxy who urges a traditionalist to develop within his tradition.

What we do when we are under the aspect of eternity, therefore, will depend upon who we are. It is a matter of our personal characteristics. What happens will depend primarily upon not only who we are, but also upon the nature of the ultimate, and how we are related to each other. As far as its nature is concerned, all that needs to be said here is that every spiritual tradition that I know bears witness that the ultimate is not inactive. There is no universal agreement on how it acts, and in what circumstances. It may "act", for example, only as beauty does, by attracting, by being attractive, or as gravitation does, or the laws of thermodynamics. But an understanding of how the ultimate acts is less important, at this stage in our living, than our understanding that apparently it is not inactive or unresponsive.

Long experience by many persons indicates that even a high degree of receptivity on our part does not guarantee that the ultimate will make itself known to us at the times we prepare for its coming. It seems to operate by its own rules and, by our human standards, not infrequently its responses appear to be governed by whim. Is the consummation delayed because of a fault in us, or for a purpose we cannot yet discern? We do not know, and most of the time it is not our business to know. Knowing is fundamentally, if not strictly, a solitary state, meeting a mutual act which depends only partially upon what we know and do not know, or do and leave undone. Again the analogy with art can be instructive. "If you would hear the Muse", writes George Moore, "you must prepare silent hours for her", and Charles Morgan adds, "They must be not silent only, but submissive. You must not question her or be impatient of her absence".[3]

Hours? Who except a professional devotee can spend hours waiting for the ultimate to manifest itself? But there is no need to wait idly. Surrender of the spirit means no more than being ready to come when we are called. Hurrying home through rush-hour traffic, we happen to see a boy and a girl smile at each other, and for a block or two we carry a glow of wonder within us from seeing their joy. While we are making a bed, a presence descends upon us; for the few minutes of its duration, we lean against the wall, savoring it. The discipline is no more burdensome than being ready to answer the telephone or doorbell. Normally we go about our business, neither sitting with hands folded beside the instrument or the door, nor tensely alert for the sound. But we are only superficially surprised when we are summoned.

A common signal of the approach of the ultimate is a heightening of our ordinary experience, an intensification of wonder, longing, stillness, peace, joy, anticipation, or of dread, penitence, fear. A presence pierces us, satisfying our hunger for personal encounter at the deepest level, and stretching our capacity to receive it. Most likely there will be no voice, no vision, no touch, but simply the sense of being met in an encounter that confirms us as persons and enlarges our personal nature. Unlike the "mind-expanding" experiences induced by drugs or violent lights or sounds, in which the self is apparently overwhelmed and its boundaries are dissolved, the meeting with the ultimate confirms the integrity of the self, while impregnating it with a new quality of life. The event is penetrating rather than sensational, and it is not our ideas that are changed but our veritable selves.

Those words are too definite, too restrictive, to convey an accurate impression of what is going on; or they are not definite enough, not sufficiently clear, for reasons that spring from the limitations of our language. "Language is based upon an observation of appearances, whereas reality is that which transcends appearances".[4] Moreover, my description here is limited

76

to only one type of encounter. I believe it to be typical, but I do not know. I am fairly sure, however, that for the most part (and with at least one notable kind of exception), our earliest encounters are not unmistakably with an ultimate at all. Either we are not adequately sensitive, in the beginning, to the distinction between the merely distant and the authentically ultimate, or the ultimate tempers its self-disclosure to our spiritual inexperience.

The exception seems to occur most often in childhood or adolescence: it is a startling, often isolated event with marked similarities to the classic mystical ecstasy. How often these juvenescent experiences occur is a matter for speculation. Reports of them are found more clearly in poetry and fiction than in psychological literature or studies in religious development, for at least one very good reason, and there may be others. Most children learn even before they enter school that any claim to an extraordinary experience leads promptly to ridicule, denial, punishment, or other unpleasant consequences, so they wisely keep silent if they see the equivalent of a burning bush, or hear what sounds like the utterance of angels.

As we welcome the first intimations of the ultimate, not snatching at them or prematurely pinning them down with dogmas, we grow more subtle in our appreciation and more exact in our responses. Over months and years, we learn how to prepare ourselves for the invasion of the ultimate, and master the skills of receptive waiting. There may be periods of weeks or of many years when every slightest motion toward welcoming the gift is answered in abundance. There may be other periods when nothing we can do evokes its presence. We are abandoned to silence and des-

olation, or to the states that St John of the Cross identified as the Dark Night of the Senses and the Dark
Night of the Soul. Then we wait—not vacantly, not
impatiently, neither blaming ourselves nor railing
against the ultimate, but steadily doing whatever jobs
we have to do, active in mind and body, our spirits
sleeping or, in some cases, in torment.

No doubt one who so wished could chart the seasons
of our poverty and plenty to discover the rhythm of
the going and coming of the presence. But I see nothing of any value for the life of the spirit that would
be achieved by such a report. To know a friend's daily
schedule of waking, working, and sleeping does not
bring us closer to him, especially since "normal"
schedules can be as flexible as weather patterns. If a
friend absents himself from us, his reasons may have
nothing whatsoever to do with our friendship—or
everything: perhaps he trusts our faithfulness so implicitly that he can go about his other business freely,
untrammeled by our importunities. Similarly, the ultimate may not have an inflexible rhythm, but may
adapt its movements to a total situation of which we
are only a part. To complicate the relation further:
although usually we know what we want, rarely do we
know what we need, especially in the spiritual realm.
Often we are like a honey-bee caught indoors and
trapped in a jar while it is being taken out to be re-
leased. Not seeing the end that is prepared for it, it
fumes at the conditions being imposed for its joy.
　The ultimate does not explain itself to us. It does
not give us reasons for the restrictions it imposes upon
us. It does not show us a map of the route we should
take, or a portrait of what it is inviting us to become,

or a list of the sacrifices and rewards that will be involved so that we can count the costs and budget our resources. From the reports we have, its most important effect is not to alter our beliefs, perfect our motives, remedy our faults, or grant us our desires—much less to ensure that we shall be happy and comfortable—but to change our essential selves. And if we were told in advance what changes were to be effected in us, we could not comprehend them, any more than a little girl whose heart is set on a new dress can comprehend becoming the kind of person who is far more concerned with her children than with her clothes.

Consequently, if we submit ourselves to the ultimate, we do so blindly. We open ourselves to an unknown, and give ourselves into its hands to do with us what it wills in its own time, its own way, and to its own unimaginable ends. Its ways are not our ways; neither are its "thoughts" our thoughts. Why, then, do we give ourselves to it? For the sake of the occasional moment, the brief season, the enduring state, when we are simultaneously awakened and satisfied at a depth that nothing else can penetrate, the moments in which we apprehend that "there are certain eternal achievements that make even happiness look like trash".[5]

At the outset we cannot give ourselves entirely to the ultimate. The complete surrender is not accomplished by an instantaneous, conscious act. There are too many levels of our being which we are not aware of at any given time, and which must be placed under obedience successively as they emerge into consciousness. Like a soldier taking his oath to follow orders, or a man and woman pledging themselves to each other in marriage, we can decide at one time, in one act, to live *sub specie aeternitatis*. But as the orders still have to be obeyed one by one and the marital vows reaffirmed in unexpected details, so the life of the spirit must be lived in specific circumstances.

If the requirements of military or marital life become too arduous, we can refuse to re-enlist or get a divorce, and if the ultimate lays more of a burden upon us than we are willing to carry, we can revoke our commitment to it—although not, it seems, at every stage on our journey, and not always with impunity. To understand why, we must analyze more precisely what goes on in the encounter with the ultimate.

To repeat: first of all, it is a personal encounter. We respond as persons, which is to say as beings who are at once social and individual, living together in a world of which we all are a part. Second, what approaches us in the experience of wonder, and what we kneel to in worship, is other than mundane. It is final, absolute, transcendent, of a kind different from the natural world of our ordinary lives. Third, entering us, it expands and deepens the personhood that was generated in our natural contacts with other persons and things. And fourth, as we surrender increasingly to the ultimate, the invasion becomes an impregnation, and from the union of the finite person with the infinite ultimate is born a new life, a new mode of living as distinct from personal life as the personal is distinct from the merely biological, and the biological from merely physical existence.

I appropriate the term "spiritual" for this new kind of life, and "spirit" for the new kind of being, not because I believe that this is what the words have meant historically in every case. Our forebears did not always cleanly differentiate "spirit" from "person". I believe, however, that my use is continuous with theirs, so that such phrases as "the spirit of the mountain" can properly be interpreted as "that aspect of the mountain which encourages us to see it under the aspect of eternity", and in Christian theology, the Holy Spirit can be understood as the power by which (or more accurately, the person by whom) all nature is, or can be, impregnated with the divine life and so can become spiritual.

We can refuse the proffered gift and still be good and even great persons. We might say that the axis and abscissa of personal development are good and evil, magnificence and pettiness, and for the most part these are under our control. The poles of spiritual development are the holy and the fiendish; they constitute another dimension. And holiness is not under our control in any sense whatsoever.

We can degrade the spirit; we cannot create ourselves as spiritual beings or spread our progress toward sanctity except indirectly, because becoming holy is a gift, not an achievement. The apprentice can interfere with the master-craftsman and spoil his work. Upon occasion, he can help by handing tools to his master. But one of the first things the beginner needs to learn is when to keep out of the way. Later, as a journeyman, he can safely do more: he is then beyond the need for primers and can initiate some projects of his own, as well as give a hand with the masterpiece under his master's direction. That stage, however, lies well beyond any point we shall reach in this book.

In the first movement of surrender, we open ourselves

to the invasion of the ultimate. In the second we offer it our concerns. We present to it a person (another or others or ourselves), a situation, an activity, a thing, not asking that this or that be done, but lifting it *sub specie aeternitatis* as a gardener moves a potted plant into the sun. Already, of course, whatever we are concerned about exists under the aspect of eternity; in one sense, therefore, our offering accomplishes nothing. In another sense, when we invite the ultimate to penetrate another person or a state of affairs, we construct a channel to facilitate its invasion. It is as if sometimes the ultimate exhibits the courtesy of waiting for our invitation before it intervenes in our affairs.

"Take it—take him or her or them or me—and do what Thou wilt." Then we have done almost all that we can do by way of offering and intercession. There may or may not follow what the Quakers call a "leading" that we should bestir ourselves within that situation. It has been said that we should never pray for a situation where we are not prepared to act, but why should we not pray when there is nothing else that we can do—when we are unable to act in any other way? Why should we suppose that the ultimate has no other or better instruments than we are to convey what the problem needs for its ultimate solution? Possibly our busy-ness has contributed to the crisis, so that our best service will be to keep our meddling hands out of it. Any number of times we make a path straight and smooth for the coming of the ultimate, and it comes not to us but to someone else. Was our effort, then, in vain? Not if we are centrally concerned with obedience. "Usually the way must be made ready for heaven", writes Charles Williams, "and then it will come by some other; the sacrifice must be made ready, and the fire will strike on another altar".[6]

In the practice of intercession, the notion of "an answer to prayer" becomes almost completely empty of meaning. We may not have raised any questions. We have not necessarily begged any favors or tried to shift the course of events. Nothing in our prayer needs to have called for any form of answer from the ultimate, because what we have done is primarily only to reaffirm, in a specific instance, what we take to be a general fact: that all persons and states of affairs exist under the aspect of eternity. What had been a tacit understanding is made an explicit proclamation in the hope, if not the confidence, that the action of the ultimate may thereby be facilitated. Not in passive resignation, but in creative acceptance, we wait upon the Lord, or whatever it is that fulfils for us the function which some people call by that name.

By definition, both natural prayer and the prayer to the ultimate are directed toward an other. The worshipper is not trying to rule himself or to do something by himself. He is engaged in relating a finite reality effectively to a final reality. In natural prayer the desired effect is to elicit a response from another, and in prayer to the ultimate, a surrender to another. Either way, two poles are predicated, in contrast with the programs of self-mastery advocated in the rational disciplines of humanism, in some schools of psychology, and in certain of the esoteric cults. Within the framework of prayer many modifications are possible, from praise to repentance to supplication, but always with the double reference to the self and to the ultimate not-self, each defined in terms of the other, and each redefined progressively as their relation matures.

Does this "other" really exist? How we answer that question depends not upon abstract philosophical demonstration, but upon a personal commitment. Before we can fruitfully investigate the nature of the ultimate, we must become acquainted with it, and neither the first nor the last analysis will be adequate unless it takes full account of the fact that when we encounter the ultimate, it appears to be other than ourselves. Some appearances do lie: on a hot, sunny day, the road ahead of us appears to be wet but it is not. Some appearances, however, do reflect reality: the curve in the road looks sharp, and we regain consciousness in the ambulance knowing by our shattered bodies that the appearance was truer than we had credited it with being. Until we have explored the life of the spirit by exercising imaginative appreciation and practical discipline, we are in no position to make an intellectual—much less an intelligent—appraisal of it.

A final word about our approach to the ultimate: let us take it seriously but also lightly. An instructive story, probably apocryphal, is told of an experienced spiritual director who was counselling a society matron. She had set herself the discipline of thinking about God the very first moment when she woke up in the morning, a practice that has been widely taught through the centuries as indispensable for setting the tone of the entire day. For months she had worked to establish that habit, to no avail, and finally, in the midst of one of her interminable lamentations, her spiritual director gave up. "My dear madam," he said, "the first thing *I* think of when I wake up is whether I can get to the bathroom before I wet my pajamas".

We are embodied persons, beset with physical urgencies of many kinds which keep intruding upon even our most exalted moments. We hunger; we suffer from arthritis, indigestion, heat and cold, varicose veins. When I read of someone who reports having knelt in prayer for a week, or only a day, without rising from his knees, I begin to wonder. Conceivably all his bodily functions were suspended except for his circulation and breathing, and these were diminished (Teresa of Avila was taken to be dead during at least one of her transports), but for such a length of time? It seems more realistic to suppose that the worshipper continued praying while he attended to his bodily needs. He may indeed have blessed them, in terms such as Aron quotes from "a collection of one hundred blessings ... [that] was certainly in use at the time of Jesus' birth":[7] "Blessed art thou, O Lord our God, King of the universe, who has formed man in wisdom, and created in him many passages and vessels".[8] Or the worshipper may have been in a trance state. My own suspicion is that the people who report such uninterrupted states have taken the intervals when they attended to their bodies as if they were rests between movements of a symphony, which do not count as breaks in the music. In fact, the author of *The Cloud of Unknowing* says as much:

> . . . you must realize that in this life it will be
> impossible to continue in this work with the
> same intensity all the time. Sickness,
> afflictions of body and mind, and countless
> other necessities of nature will often leave you

indisposed and keep you from its heights. Yet, at the same time, I counsel you to remain at it always either in earnest or, as it were, playfully. What I mean is that through desire, you can remain with it even when other things intervene.[9]

Our bodies are not only fearfully and wonderfully made, but in some lights ridiculous. Correspondingy, there is more than a little to ridicule in the notion that a finite and otherwise imperfect being could be in touch with ultimate perfection. It is material for farce, and we lose something of its glory if we fail to enjoy its absurdity. The fool of God, the clown laughing and dancing before the altar or on it, or stripping to plunge into the surf, or kicking his heels in the courts of the Most High or in the fetid air of a primitive hospital, is one of the most sacred of all images. He mocks our inordinate solemnities and entices us out of our self-importance. He reminds us to glory in the foolishness of our humanity, to be happy, to laugh, to kick up *our* heels upon occasion with the abandon of a lamb, a colt, a kid, a clown. Our spiritual life is incomplete without him.

Even in strictly human relationships, it is a good rule to take it easy, not to force things, not to hurry, but to enjoy the slow ripening of a friendship or love. All the more, our relation with the ultimate develops at its own pace, seasons of laughter alternating with seasons of intensity and of indifference. They are all part of the process and of the pattern, all to be welcomed as aspects of the breakthrough of the barriers between us and the utterly transcendant. Prayer can be a kind of play, and play a form of prayer as when human lovers are drawn to each other in sharing ribald jokes and mischievous games. In many religions, feasting and gaiety have as important a part to play in spiritual life as fasting and gravity. Charles Williams, writing from within the Christian tradition, says,

> Relaxation is no less holy and proper than rigour, though perhaps it can hardly be preached so. But the lovely refreshments of this world in some may not be without their part in the lordly rigours of others; . . . if we thrive by the force of the saints, they too may feed on our felicities.[10]

CHAPTER FOUR

Ways of Praying

> *In a general way . . . the high Omnipotence*
> *confines its direction precisely to the immediate next*
> *step, and does not always make that very clear.*
>
> Charles Williams
> *Flecker of Dean Close*

"Thou art there. I am here". Or "I am here, thou art here". Once we are under the aspect of eternity, what are we going to do?

Much depends upon why we have come here, how we were impelled to fall on our knees. We begin where we are, which is not in a vacuum but in a context, and that context differs for each person and at different moments. Thus to ask whether our first act should be to praise or repent, to intercede or to protest, is to raise an unanswerable question. We should do what is appropriate to *our* occasion. Presumably even an invocation such as "Almighty God", or clapping one's hands or ringing a bell or otherwise calling upon the ultimate, is unnecessary, helpful though it may be in focusing our attention and continuing our concentration.

The time may come when we develop a ritual for our worship, but we should neither seek for nor resist that outcome. Rituals are only instruments, and no two persons will use quite the same ones in their private devotions. Masters in the life of the spirit like Teresa of Avila, Ignatius Loyola, François de Sales, and Baron von Hügel, can prescribe detailed exercises partly because they are working with persons who are already advanced toward spiritual maturity, and who have decided to undergo the special disciplines of formation. They have found their métier.

But this book is written for persons who have not yet discovered theirs. They—we—are still experimenting with forms and styles, learning how the tools fit our hands and whether we are more comfortable employing the chisel, the brush, or the spade. It could be said that we are playing around, although it is play with the serious intention of developing skills, learning what the various tools can and cannot do, and if necessary inventing new tools and techniques. Or in a simpler metaphor, we are at the stage of trying on shoes, rather than of setting off on an extended walking tour.

The notes that follow, therefore, are intended to do no more than suggest a few of the basic ways for exploring and experimenting, with no warnings or promptings except one: that the novice should look forward to giving most of them a trial at some time or other as circumstances suggest, not forcing himself to do so, and not hurrying to get through a list, but keeping in mind a wide range of possibilities so that when he needs a particular tool, he will know what is available.

The occasions and motives for prayer are multitudinous. For convenience, I group them according to very general human conditions, which among them cover a great many of the circumstances when we especially want to pray: when our hearts are full, or empty, or divided.

Our hearts are over-urdened with a weight of glory or of pain, and we need to be relieved of that heaviness. The simple urge to share a momentous occurrence, lest we explode from the internal pressure, can often be satisfied by exulting or lamenting or admitting our guilt to another person. Such a person can enter into our experience and receive its overflow, at once easing us of its intensity and confirming its importance to us. Even the most sympathetic human response, however, will sometimes be inadequate for the greatness of our need, too shallow for its depth. Or no one may be at hand who can serve as a safety-valve. Then our passion divides us from the rest of mankind and perhaps even from nature. We are isolated by our rapture or grief or shame. At that juncture, our cry goes out beyond the world, "This is more than I can bear alone. Bear it with me".

The joy is not taken from us. The grief may not be removed or the physical agony alleviated. Instead, we are enlarged by this sharing with the ultimate. Our capacity to endure is increased. Not infinitely—we do not become gods by giving ourselves to the ultimate or by putting our affairs into its hands. More precisely, when by prayer we confirm that these events and our reactions to them stand within a frame of reference which is ultimate, we begin to participate in a mode of being that transcends the merely human and the mundane. When my sorrow and bliss and shame belong not just to me, and not just to you and me, but also are held within the ultimate, their intensity no longer isolates me from the whole of the universe, but becomes a strong cord binding me to all that is. As the ultimate shares my stress, I become capable of sharing it with other persons.

That sharing, whether *sub specie aeternitatis* or *sub specie temporis*, involves both giving and receiving. We address the ultimate, saying in effect, "Take it and do with it what Thou wilt". What happens then can best be exhibited by examples that are to be understood as suggestive or indicative, not as models to be imitated; and in order to emphasize that limitation, I cast them in the first person singular.

I am in a public restaurant when I am swept by a flood of awareness: every face that I see is radiant with its individuality. Even the glum and the apparently apathetic are "apparelled in celestial light".[1] During that moment I love them passionately, each one of all these strangers. I cannot express my love directly: they would be embarrassed or would resent my intruding upon their privacy. But I can offer my surge of love to the ultimate for it to use. "Give the energy of my love to someone who needs it". Thus my love enters the limitless transactions of life, and I am joined not only with the ultimate, but to every person who may have received my gift, and especially to whoever

91

presumably did. I have no idea how or when or to whom the gift is given, and no evidence that it is used at all—as if evidence were important.

In contrast, I lie awake for hours, enduring silently a critical anxiety attack, saturated, engorged with that peculiar kind of anguish. Feeling that I cannot live through another minute of it, still I continue to live, and finally it occurs to me that since I am having to put up with my private anxiety, and apparently have not quite reached the limit of my endurance, I may as well bear part of someone else's anxiety while I am at it. With that intention, although not with words, I invite the ultimate to let me carry another person's anxiety along with my own. That burden is added to mine, and the ultimate carries us both until, very shortly, I fall peacefully to sleep.

At a dinner party I make an unnecessary, nasty remark which even at the time I am ashamed of, but the topic of conversation changes before I can retract it. To apologize later would require a long-distance call or a letter, either of which would inflate the incident out of all reasonable proportion. Prostrated with contrition, I offer the whole situation to the ultimate with the urgent desire that my evil may serve some good end. Off and on for a long time I wonder what good has come of that evil, but I have never learned.

Hearing of a mountaineer who has been separated from his party in a storm, I find myself obsessed by the image of my hands holding him and lifting him into the light of the ultimate—almost like a child bringing a broken doll for her mother to mend. I do not know if the climber is alive or dead, and if the safety I seem to be offering him be physical deliverance or deliverance of some other kind, but I keep on even after the rescue teams have given up, until days later he stumbles into a campground, weak but alive.

Such prayers to the ultimate are almost always inconclusive. Nothing seems to happen when we pray in this manner unless perhaps—and incidentally—that our imaginations are activated. Can we, by our prayers, directly alleviate a stranger's anxiety, help to redeem our sins, save a person who is in danger, give joy to somebody or other? Who knows? Why should we care? What they do accomplish, unmistakably, is to place ourselves at the disposal of the ultimate. What it does with what we have given it is not our work and none of our business. As in the Buddhist and Shinto rituals of venerating ancestors, nothing identifiable is supposed to happen directly and concretely. Our forces are united with other forces not to increase our effectiveness or to achieve a defined purpose, but to liberate and intensify the work of the ultimate in the world. If evidence be required, all we can present is our experience that now we live from a new root and see with new eyes—a claim that cannot be verified or falsified by any methods that I know anything about.

To the disinterested eye, life under the aspect of the mundane and life under the aspect of eternity may not visibly differ, and their disparity may not be measurable by psychological or other tests. All the same, what is done under the one aegis differs as profoundly from what is done under the other as the mundane differs from the ultimate.

Our hearts are empty, deserts under a vacant sky, and we hunger and thirst to be filled. All about us lies the spring of the year, but we have no part in its burgeoning. Our customary rituals have gone dead on us. The friends and books and music we once found nourishing are sawdust in our mouth. Yesterday the intimations of ultimacy were strong within us; today the sky is merely the sky instead of a veil over the face of the most high, and we feel not only destitute but betrayed.

Here, of all places, we are most likely to resort to natural prayer. "Come back to me ... Show thyself again ... Cast me not away from thy presence". By every technique at our command, we attempt to compel the return of that presence. We redouble the performance of familiar rites, undertake special disciplines of meditation and behavior, seek new words and postures for worship. Natural prayers may achieve the result we desire. But also, they may not, and we may be too empty even for the desire to germinate. Or we may have learned earlier in our spiritual life not to interfere with the motions of the ultimate toward us, because its silences are for a purpose, and even its apparent absence is a form of its presence. For days clouds have covered the sky: do we therefore conclude that our prior perceptions of the sun and moon were illusions? Although it may require a sturdy act of faith to trust that the sun will shine again and that the ultimate will again manifest itself, the periods of dullness need not be wasted. Certain activities are more appropriate for dreary weather inside ourselves or outdoors than for fine seasons—like cleaning closets. For example, and again framing the examples as if they had happened to me:

A friend confides to me a grave and urgent problem, and while we are struggling for a solution to it, I inwardly pray that we may see it in the light of the ultimate and so learn what will be the best course of action for her. No such illumination is forthcoming, and she leaves in at least as much confusion as she arrived. Several negative interpretations are possible: that we were too blind to see ... that the ultimate was indifferent ... that the darkness represented a punishment for our sins ... that we had not yet worked hard enough on the problem to have earned light. More positively, we might conclude that the confusion postponed action in a situation that was not yet ripe for her to act ... that I was calling for "divine guidance" in a circumstance where our natural resources of mind and body were sufficient, but we were not using them ... that I had prayed in cowardice or laziness for a help that we did not really need.

For many months I battle in an almost suicidal depression to adapt myself to a deprivation which I shall have to live with for the rest of my life. Intellectually, I am convinced that eternally all shall be well, but I cannot bring myself even to the point of wanting to see it in that light. My intellect is impotent to curb my resentment; my spirit is dumb or dead. I come through because I fasten the remaining shreds of my determination to the certainty that experiences do not cancel each other out. Once I had lived under the aspect of eternity; my current darkness does not signify that the earlier knowledge of joy was an illusion. Morever, while I am utterly outside joy, I can see that it still inhabits others, and now and then by a spoken or written word, news comes that the ultimate still reveals itself, even though not to me. Because my emptiness is only mine, and not an epidemic disease afflicting all the rest of the world, I can rejoice for the others even though not—for the time being—with them.

So also during the frequent periods when I feel abandoned for no discernible reason. Those are times for the exercise of intellect and determination while the spirit sleeps and, sleeping, grows like a child in its mother's womb—or at least such is my hope. It seems as if I am forbidden to live only by the spirit, as if nature (body, mind, heart) has its essential part in spiritual development. If I neglect them, those natural functions will grow flabby and coarse, unfitted for their necessary part in the development of the person who prays.

According to one great tradition of spiritual life, the ultimate informs nature; therefore natural processes must be fostered or the spirit will not have good material to work with. According to another tradition, spirit replaces nature; therefore natural processes must decrease and eventually perish. The procedures recommended for dealing with emptiness, however, are virtually the same in both cases.

In all the great traditions, the novice is warned to expect such intervals. He is taught to endure them patiently when they come, neither trying to fight his way out nor succumbing listlessly to them. Probably he will be instructed to discipline himself while they last—in one case, by intellectual studies and physical work, in the other by practices designed to curb thinking and activity. His body may be subjected to athletic or ascetic control, depending upon the goal that is envisioned and, in some cases, by what has been found most helpful to him individually. The times of emptiness can be times for coming to terms with the mundane, both within and outside ourselves, whether the goal is a potentially fruitful union of differences, as between male and female, or a victory of one value

over another, as of good over evil. George Mac-
Donald's advice is as sound today as it was when he
wrote it more than a century ago: "Troubled soul,
thou art not bound to feel, but though art bound to
arise.... Bethink thee of something that thou oughtest
to do, and go and do it, if it be but the sweeping of
a room, or the preparing of a meal, or a visit to a friend.
Heed not thy feelings: Do thy work".[2]

Our hearts are divided and we yearn to be whole. We
begin to pray, and a flood of distractions rushes
through our minds. We prepare to act, and find ourselves motivated to move in diametrically opposed directions. Having bowed before the ultimate, we start
questioning, arguing, demanding explanations. We
are fractured by doubt or by the inability to determine
what is right, or we rage against the ultimate because
of what it permits—or sends: wars, holocausts,
plagues, public and private injustices ... a comprehensive list would be endless. Should we remonstrate
against the ways of God to men? We do. Should we
be double-minded? We are, and we cannot, by des-
potic measures, acquire for ourselves that purity of
heart which, according to Kierkegaard, is to will one
thing. Our problem, therefore, is not whether we
should protest to the ultimate, or whether we should
consent to be disintegrated, but how we can use these
natural reactions and states to further the life of the
spirit.
    We are divided from the ultimate: "Why did you
let this happen? ... Why don't you stop it?" The
"Thou" of reverence or intimacy is gone. So also is
the cautious disposition to placate the ultimate by stoical submission. Our anger is too vehement for us to

focus it on a human target. Our antagonist is the universe and whatever lies beyond or beneath it, and we demand a reply. Our posture, in awaiting that reply, is one of challenge rather than of openness, yet as long as we believe that an answer may be given, the challenge will be without pride. Then, having stated our case, we are duty bound to listen for a response.

Openness here can consist of probing: "Is this the reason, or this or this or that?" Some interpretations appease our hearts but offend our intellects. Some are mentally but not emotionally adequate. Some satisfy us wholly, but only for a short time and others not at all. Each is a sign, a leading: "Dead End". "Proceed with Caution". "Resume Speed". Each such directive helps us to prepare for hearing the response from the ultimate when it is given and, having heard, to accept it—remembering that while acceptance may come with perception in a flash of joy, it may also happen that accepting the gift will be more difficult than recognizing it.

Or we are divided within ourselves, fragmented, disintegrated. "I know what I ought to do, and I want to do it, but I can't": to keep my temper ... to say that I'm sorry ... to get on with the job ... to give up the indulgence ... to turn from one way of life to another. There are too many strings tying us, strings of habit, of responsibility, of people who expect us to be always the same and whose expectations hamper our impetus toward change. Because our lives are not entirely under our control, we cannot be sure that our motives are as pure as we hope, or as foul as we are afraid they are. Our proud intellects take to playing tricks on us, rationalizing, projecting, reifying, and

98

personifying, until we cannot pray with a single mind if at all.

Powerless to pray with integrity—wholeness, soundness—still we can pray. The part of us which desires union with the ultimate need not be silenced by the indifferent or rebellious part. "Here I am in all my confusion and division. Do with me as Thou wilt". Now especially we must be alert to discern the response from the ultimate, because it is likely to be so different from what we expect. Our dis-integrity may have to be intensified before it can be healed. The handicap that crippled us may be transformed into the cornerstone of a new building instead of being obliterated. Quite possibly nothing will happen, as far as we can tell, until after a long time and many partial submissions.

If the ultimate has any power at all, however, it can function as effectively within our divided selves as with our integrity, if we allow it to do so. And it can penetrate as deeply the depths that we are not at the moment aware of as into our conscious selves, even though we may become conscious of its activity in our hidden levels only after much of its work has been accomplished.

Where division exits within ourselves, or between us and the ultimate, we have two primary tasks. First, we need to keep our priorities clear. We may not feel like continuing in the life of the spirit, but we can choose to keep on anyway. A good deal of the time we may entirely forget about it, as a good workman or housewife will frequently forget about getting a promotion or "making a home" in order to concentrate upon what immediately needs to be done. But on the occasions when we must choose between serving the ultimate and obeying some other lord, it helps to know what the issue is. In contrast, there are the more frequent occasions when we must choose between two possibilities, both of which are spiritually important at the moment, as by visiting a friend or cleaning the house, where the question is not of ethics but of style, therefore to be handled on a different basis.

Our second task is not to interfere with what the ultimate is doing in and with us. Often we are tempted to urge the ultimate into immediate and conspicuous action. Or we want to read its mind, so to speak, in order to anticipate its judgements. Or we dally around hunting for omens in natural phenomena, guidance from our horoscopes, rules from our teachers. Through ignorance, weakness, insensitivity, defective judgement, the frivolity of trying too little or the fanaticism of trying too hard, we hamper the workings of the ultimate in ourselves, our fellows, the world.

Between frivolity and fanaticism lies a broad region with ample room for gravity and mirth, action and contemplation. If we care enough about ultimate concerns to persevere in the life of the spirit, the ultimate will progressively teach us how to detect when we are interfering with its activities.

Early in our awareness of the ultimate, some of us have a sense of being guided in specific affairs; but sooner or later the guidance becomes intermittent, and we are left to do the best we can without clear leadings. But our best turns out to be not very good. We work to increase our knowledge, improve our skills in handling ideas, develop our imaginations, refine our ethical sensitivities, discipline our behavior. We attend worship services assiduously, practise meditation regularly, increase our times for prayer. Occasionally we are warned by painful twinges, or encouraged by flashes of wonder or the awareness of a presence, which serve to define our proper boundaries as well as to clarify our goals. The attitude of doggedly making do with what we have is gradually replaced by the habitual response, "What does this look like under the aspect of eternity?", accompanied by what I can only describe as a sense of the fitness of things as we see them under the aspect of the ultimate.

We are divided from our fellows, and we yearn for community. This chapter and the preceding one may have sounded too much as if prayer were a private transaction between an individual and the ultimate. That impression is both true and false—true, because persons are individuals as well as social beings, and false because their social nature is not cancelled out in their individual undertakings.

At this period in history, the population of the world and the ease of communication have increased until privacy has become a jealously guarded treasure. Our breathing space has diminished. For many of us, no hour of the day or night is free from the possibility of intrusion. Animals and plants, when overcrowded, kill each other off or develop abnormalities. Human beings react to excessive population pressure in much the same ways. I have no doubt that in our era, many of the breakdowns in communication are caused primarily by the simple fact that we are almost never free from the pressure of other people. Mere crowding turns what might otherwise be only an irritant into an agony.

"Getting away from it all" is one of the principal

ways by which we gain the perspective and proportion that enable us to live in community without tearing at each other's throats. Separation from our fellows, dearly though we may love them, is not a luxury but an imperative, physically, psychologically, and spiritually. Obviously, too much solitude can be as destructive as too little, but in our world today, the danger of having too much is less acute than that of having too little. Unfortunately, many of us do not know how to use what solitude we can achieve, so that when in old age or illness or among strangers we are alone, we resent the necessity rather than enjoy the opportunity.

In practice, natural prayer can be used to draw us either into or out of community. Communion with the ultimate, however, even in private and focussing upon private concerns, inevitably leads to community, not as an artificial construct but as a natural result of our relation with the ultimate. If as individual persons we live under the aspect of eternity, we shall reverence all persons, ourselves and others alike, and our associations will be bound together by the flexible yet enduring ties of mutual respect. Granted, most of us are not yet individual or personal enough for such an achievement, and it may take a long time for us to find the balance between society and solitude that is right for us individually.

Early in our spiritual experiments, some of us will be impelled to go on retreat for a time, secluding ourselves mentally if we cannot leave our ordinary habitations. Others, of course, may be thrown at once by the ultimate into social activities as their way of finding or creating a desirable balance. In either case, it is likely that these initial moves will be preludes to a rhythmic interplay between social and solitary phases.

102

Thus we may develop a systematic "sabbatical" rhythm of an hour a day to ourselves, or one day a week, or a couple of weeks or a month every year. Or we may develop flexibility into a high art, taking a few minutes when they are available, and longer stretches when we are given opportunity, to escape from clutter into lucidity, and from the mundane into the transcendent. Then when we are pulled back into ordinary (or extraordinary) activities—as we shall be, one way or another—we return willingly, refreshed for companionship or struggle.

Few of the divisions within and among us can be completely healed by nothing more than a retreat devoted to worship, singly or together, but nearly all would be diminished in their scope and intensity. There remain conflicts of ideas and loyalties, natural antipathies, and other occasions for division among us. These can still be offered to the ultimate, like our joys and pains, for it to penetrate and perhaps resolve. We may or may not be called to go further: to initiate discussion of such ideas, to try to change allegiances or attitudes, to alter environments. The ultimate may enjoin us to wait, not because time itself has therapeutic powers but because most therapies take time. The advice, "Don't just do something; stand there", is co-equal with "Don't just stand there; do something", and the expectation that we ought to rise from our knees to rush frantically into action is as fatuous as the expectation that once we are on our knees, only a cataclysm will induce us to stand on our feet again, or walk or run or dance.

The ultimate does not solve for us our problems in human relations, any more than it constructs our highways or answers questions for us on the examination we are taking. It can, in time, quicken our sense of proportion and release our minds and hearts from rigidities, frailties, and confusions that impede both individual and social fulfilment. "Spirit" is no substitute for natural ability and effort; neither does it merely improve our natural faculties. Its function in nature is apparently to enable, empower, heighten, restore, lift up, raise from the dead, and its operation is indeed within and upon communities as well as individuals.

There remains the problem, endemic in our society, of loneliness. A young woman is visiting an elderly relative living alone in a small city apartment. "What do you do when you get lonely?" she asks. He replies, "I don't", and she—aching with loneliness—goes empty away.

Such emptiness can be a summons to turn away from the inadequacies of surroundings in which we are companioned only superficially, toward the supreme adequacy of the transcendent world. The hitch in the invitation is that seemingly we must consent within ourselves to be lonely in order to come out on the other side, eat the bitter fruit before biting into the sweet core, cross the desert before reaching the river of life. Loneliness throws us upon our own resources, urges (if it does not compel) us to stand on our own feet and become authentically ourselves, when we would prefer to be supported by others and have our identity conferred upon us.

Not to seek for and accept what the mundane world can give is a kind of asceticism that is rarely if ever desirable for the novice. On the other hand, there are some things that the world cannot give, although we may not be able to identify what those are until we have exhausted the mundane possibilities. And there are no short-cuts.

Historically, many types of prayer have been distinguished, and it may be useful to discuss briefly a dozen or so taken from the Christian tradition, most of which, if not all, have parallels in non-Christian traditions. As before, the references and examples are offered as illustrative, not restrictive, and with the reminder that any of them can be practised either in solitude or in company.

Meditation and contemplation are often used synonymously, but here I shall differentiate them, taking *meditation* to be a concentration upon some idea or object with the intention of seeing it under the aspect of eternity. The idea may be an event (perhaps the birth of Jesus), a word (mantra), a teaching (sutra), a prayer—what you will. The object may be a picture, a sculpture, a shell, a flower, a cup, a candle—anything you like. In meditation, we look receptively at whatever-it-is, perhaps imaginatively recreating the event, perhaps carefully observing the object. Then we use it as a lens through which the ultimate reveals itself to us in our relations with the world. Something in or of the world becomes a means by which we move beyond the world.

Sometimes we do this spontaneously, as when a person stands for minutes on end, awestruck by the majesty of a waterfall, or sits musing on a phrase that has suddenly burst open with meaning. Meditation can be as simple and natural as Avery Brooke describes in *How to Meditate without Leaving the World*, or as elaborate and systematic as Ignatius Loyola prescribes in his *Spiritual Exercises*.[3]

In *contemplation*, as I am using the term, we do not concentrate our thoughts; we empty our minds. The Quakers call it "centering down"; Basil Pennington in *Finding Grace at the Center* calls it "the prayer of quiet"; Thomas Keating, in the same book, speaks of "the centering prayer". It can also be described as a state of unfocussed awareness. Some people have taught that contemplation is an advanced stage of spirituality which must be preceded by mastering meditation. Others have said that it is an extraordinary gift bestowed upon only a very few. But it is not all that uncommon for a child to fall into a rapt absorption and, when we ask what he is thinking about, to reply with precise accuracy, "Nothing".[4] He is not merely not thinking, a negative concept; he is positively not-thinking, engaged in contemplation, and the fact that almost certainly he cannot explain what he is doing in no way prevents him from doing it.

Contemplation comes naturally to some people, as meditation to others, and one can practice both at different times. They are no more mutually exclusive than are Charles Williams' "Way of the Rejection of Images" and "Way of the Affirmation of Images",[5] although most of us seem to be drawn more strongly to one of these ways. Intrinsically, neither represents a higher type of spirituality, or requires less discipline than the other, but the disciplines are different.

Prayers of *petition* are probably what most people think of first when they think about praying. "Lighten our darkness"; "Defend us thy humble servants in all assaults of our enemies"; "Support us all the day long of this troublous life"; "Send us, we beseech thee, in this our necessity, such moderate rain and showers,

106

that we may receive the fruits of the earth to our comfort";[6] "Now I lay me down to sleep. I pray the Lord my soul to keep". Three kinds of petition, however, call for special attention.

The first is *invocation*, entreating the ultimate to be present in whatever we are particularly concerned with. "I bind unto myself today the strong name of the Trinity, by invocation of the same, the three in one and one in three";[7] "I will kindle my fire this morning / In presence of the holy angels of heaven . . . God, kindle thou in my heart within / A flame of love to my neighbor";[8] "Send out thy light and thy truth that they may lead me";[9] "O Lord, we come this morning/Knee-bowed and body-bent / Before thy throne of grace".[10]

The second is *intercession*, in which we plead for another. "We entrust all who are dear to us to thy never-failing care and love"; "Defend, O Lord, this thy child with thy heavenly grace"; "We commend to thy fatherly goodness all those who are in any ways afflicted or distressed in mind, body, or estate".[11]

Less familiar is another kind of intercession: the practice of substituted love in which one person takes over from another a fear or anger or pain or other suffering and thereby relieves the sufferer from his burden. Charles Williams is the only writer I know who has presented in detail both its theory[12] and its practice.[13] In *Descent into Hell*, a novel, he compares it with carrying a parcel, such as a bag of groceries or a piece of luggage, for someone else. "If you give a weight to me, you can't be carrying it yourself".[14] This form of intercession is more and other than simply wishing someone well. It is placing ourselves between that person and the ultimate, as a bridge. It sounds easy, but usually it is not, and the work is not to be undertaken lightly.

The third special kind of petition is *penitence*, that is, confessing one's sins and asking to be forgiven. "I have done wrong, rotten wrong, and I'm wretched about it";[15] "Forgive us our sins"; "We have erred and strayed from thy ways like lost sheep"; "We acknowledge and bewail our manifold sins and wickedness ... and grant that we may ever hereafter serve and please thee in newness of life".[16] This last clause reminds us that the purpose of penitential confession is the restoration of a relationship that we have violated, not—decidedly not—the psychological relief of venting our emotions. At issue is not what we feel but what we do, the classic three steps for restoring any relationship: looking to see what the situation is in both its brokenness and its wholeness, admitting how we have contributed to the brokenness, and doing whatever we can to restore the wholeness.

Thanksgiving can be as personal as "Thank you, God", or as impersonal as "I'm so glad that it worked out!" when the working out is seen under the aspect of eternity. Likewise, *praise* can be directed to a divine being or to "all that is". "Blessed art thou, O Lord our God, King of the universe, who makest the bonds of sleep to fall upon mine eyes, and slumber upon mine eyelids";[17] "We praise thee, O God; we acknowledge thee to be the Lord. All the earth doth worship thee";[18] "My poems are hymns of praise to the glory of Life";[19] "Praised be the fathomless universe".[20]

Our prayer can be *conversational*, as casual or passionate as talking with a friend. We tell the ultimate our problems and delights not to impart information, but as a way of placing ourselves in its presence—so to speak, of sitting down across the table from it. Essential to conversation is listening as well as speaking, and before the ultimate, we ought to listen a great deal more than most of us do. Although the ultimate rarely conveys its messages verbally, often we translate them into words, as Peguy does in *God Speaks*. And we can argue as Job did, protest, dialogue, joke, question.

Any of these prayers can be non-verbal, or (except for contemplation, which is always non-verbal) can be mentally or orally articulated. Or they can be written with anything from pencil and paper to a word processor. It may seem outlandish to write a meditation or thanksgiving or confession on a computer with word-processing capability, but if it has not yet been done, assuredly it wil be by those to whom writing is a natural medium of expression and who are at home with computers.

Reading can facilitate prayer, not only when we turn to a book of prayers so that we do not have to search for words of our own, or when others say what we mean better than we can and not only in reading scriptures of our particular religious tradition. For some of us, fiction, poetry, and essays, including some that have no direct spiritual reference, can bring us into the presence of the ultimate as nothing else does.

Finally, there are *ejaculations* such as "Help!" and "Thanks!" and "Come!" and "No!", a word or two or three drawn from us in a swift rising from the mundane to the transcendent. At the other end of the scale there is *continuous prayer*, the prototype being the so-called Jesus Prayer, most highly developed in Eastern

Orthodox Christianity, "Lord Jesus Christ, have mercy upon me (or us)," repeated incessantly during all waking hours and even during sleep, whatever one is doing: working, playing, resting, reading, eating, conversing, or anything else.[21]

At the times when we cannot pray at all because of sorrow, frustration, exhaustion, intense pain, or for any other reason, we can make these our prayer by giving them up into the ultimate. Indeed, any activity or state can function as prayer in this way, by placing it under the aspect of eternity, thus leaving us free to concentrate on whatever we are doing: fishing, gardening, playing with a child, listening to a concert, working out a thorny mathematical or sewing or architectural design problem, weeping for the dead, enduring an all-encompassing agony.

The fundamental motions of wonder and worship become coordinated into acts in much the same way that a child's apparently aimless muscular activities prepare for the coordinations of walking. So far, we are only learning to stand upright, to move forward without tumbling too often, and—we hope—developing the courage to get up after we have fallen in order to try again. How long will it take? Some children learn to walk early and quickly, others late and slowly. A few, because of accidental or inherited defect, never learn to walk at all. In some parts of the world, babies are deliberately mutilated to prevent them from ever walking normally because that way they are more effective as beggars. Likewise, the capacity for wonder can, in theory, be lacking. Certainly children and adults can be taught to inhibit wonder, or not to move from wonder to worship. The native capacity to wonder, however, is probably at least as common as the native capacity to walk, and if we can walk, we can look forward confidently to running and dancing. And when we are reasonably firm on our feet, we can begin to consider seriously what direction we shall take, along what road we shall walk and to what end.

CHAPTER FIVE

Enablements of Prayer

The road to Damascus had been illumined for the young man Saul by a lightning flash. The road from Damascus he had to build for himself.

Sholem Asch
The Apostle

Every method or circumstance that enables prayer for one person can be an impediment for him at another time, or for another person at any time. One of Richter's cartoons shows a couple gazing at a splendid vista; she is saying to him, "Whenever *you're* ready, dear. My spirit has been renewed enough".[1] C. S. Lewis writes, "I believe that many who find that 'nothing happens' when they sit down, or kneel down,

112

to a book of devotion, would find that the heart sings unbidden while they are working their way through a tough bit of theology with a pipe in their teeth and a pencil in their hand".[2] Augustine of Hippo confesses that in services of worship, he is sometimes "more moved by the singing than by the thing that is sung"[3]: music can distract from worship, or facilitate it, depending on the characteristics of the person, the situation, and doubtless the kind and quality of the words and music.

The rule is not that there are no rules but that they must be applied perceptively and intelligently. So if, for example, we are seeking a style of public worship that will be congenial, our investigation will have at least two phases. We shall want to observe and—as far as we can—participate in services of the kind we are considering, exercising our sympathy more than our critical abilities. But before or after, we shall want to study both the rite and its meaning, employing the full scope of our analytic intelligence, as well as our imaginations. I prefer to look first and study later; otherwise I tend too much to see things through other people's eyes or hear through others' ears, as I might on hearing a piece of music analyzed before I have heard it played. Some of my friends much prefer to study first and participate later. Both procedures are called for; the order that we take them can be our own.

Most of the enablements of prayer come in pairs, and generally function best when they are kept in balance—although "balance" does not mean, for example, one hour of study and one of physical labor for every hour of private devotions. The achievement is not all that simple because we are not all that simple.

The physical act of kneeling may be repugnant because we are loath to confirm an intellectual conviction with a bodily act; or perhaps because the act is sufficiently unfamiliar that we are embarrassed by performing it even in private; or merely because our knees hurt when we do. What place, then, should kneeling have in our peculiar equilibrium of body and spirit? Shall we practise kneeling as a discipline, undertake it as a way of enlarging our experience, avoid it out of respect for our ailing joints, or dismiss the whole matter as too minor to worry about?

These are all legitimate possibilities, including—if not especially—the last. Because authentic spiritual life has a very wide range of permissible variation, almost any idea or technique that is properly of supreme importance to one person will be, and should be, insignificant to someone else. In the early phases of spiritual development, we have not yet learned what is for us major and minor, so we are likely to pay undue attention to details—not a serious error unless it becomes a settled habit of mind and we fall into the sin of scrupulosity.

Corporate and solitary prayer are mutually interdependent. A prayerful gathering of persons who do not pray privately is like an orchestra whose members never touch their instruments between concerts. A person who never joins his fellows in corporate worship is like a musician who plays only by himself, forsaking the disciplines and fulfilments that are found in playing with an accompanist or an ensemble. His musicianship may be superb, but it is limited. In Charles Williams' words (although changing the tenses), "No mind is so good that it does not need another mind to counter and equal it, and to save it from conceit and blindness and bigotry and folly".[4]

Because the disciplines of the spirit are so much a matter of individual style, we may not be able to worship with every religious community available to us, even those that are of the same theological persuasion as ours. Certain forms of devotion cramp my spirit, and a few repel me. Attending services in churches, temples, or shrines that use such forms becomes for me a strenuous exercise in containing my boredom or rage. I may have every confidence in the other worshippers' sincerity and agree with their beliefs. Still, this is the wrong place for me and I had better find another.

And when I have found a group where I feel spiritually at home, other problems will arise. How often should I attend the services? As often as is necessary to keep me aware of belonging to a community of worshippers; beyond that, as often as I want or need the nourishment, correction, and pleasure of participating openly with that community. How can I tell whether the others are there to worship, or out of a dry sense of duty? I cannot, but it is only courteous to assume that they have come for the same good reasons that I come—or for better ones. Perhaps it is in order to be assured that we are not isolated in our search or to rectify our private aberrations, or to hear what we do not hear spoken publicly elsewhere.

Whether in the fire-burning ceremony at a Shinto shrine, a Liberian truth-finding ordeal, or a Christian Sunday service, public worship confronts us with an authority that claims to be final not only for us indi-

115

vidually but also for a community that transcends the place and time and individuality of this gathering: the authority of the ultimate.

There are, of course, reasons other than spiritual nurture for participating in corporate worship, but they need not concern us here. We live on many levels simultaneously, but we cannot talk about all of them at once, and ordinarily we achieve proportion by emphasizing one level and then, successively, another and another, rather than by trying to perform all our functions at once. Our immediate concern is with the worshiping community not with learning or working or socializing communities, whether they be under ecclesiastical or secular patronage. The spiritual life does lead us beyond ourselves, but *where* the Spirit wishes to lead us, and whether singly or in association, we shall not know until we give the intrinsic nature of worship more than cursory attention.

There are, of course, situations—in travelling, for instance—in which we are cut off from any group with which we have fellow-feeling with respect to the ultimate. And there are times when we cannot, or should not, release ourselves into union with others. If at a Thanksgiving celebration we are consumed by a private grief, we ought to conceal it for the sake of the others. If in a rigidly formal rite our hearts move spontaneously in another direction, we can preserve the amenities while inwardly we take another road. Our consciousness that we belong to a community of faith which is gathered from all times and places may be more strongly realized when we are in solitude than in a crowded cathedral. And we may be more acutely aware of our private confrontation with the ultimate while we are attending a mass revival meeting than when we are closeted in our bedroom.

The ways by which the ultimate leads us into balance can be strange, as in some of the preceding examples, as well as in the cases where an individual over-emphasizes one style in his own life as a counterbalance to excessive stress upon the other in the society where he happens to live. It is tempting to suggest that ideally, every person will attain a standard proportion between corporate and solitary worship in his own life, but that temptation is toward spiritual dullness. The ideal we should strive for is obedience, which can very well mean markedly different styles even for husband and wife, or for one child in a family and all the other members of that family.

We cannot prescribe for another beyond urging that each follow the leading given to him, and helping him test that leading against the experience of others. But we had better be certain what spirit is directing us— divine or mundane or fiendish—if, having embarked on the life of the spirit, we totally exclude either private or corporate worship except as a temporary expedient during a special crisis or phase of our development or—like some of the hermits—as a compensation for a prevailing disposition in our time.

Shall we pray with or without a prearranged order of worship, whether in corporate or solitary devotions? Is it better to wait passively for "the leading of the spirit", or to plan a ritual for actively approaching its presence? These two methods, the extemporaneous and the organized, exhibit different ways of handling one of the most common problems in spiritual discipline: concentration. We have settled down for half an hour of meditation or prayer, and we remember an item that must go on the shopping list. The telephone rings. Our minds drift to an event that happened yesterday, an appointment tomorrow, an item in the newspaper, a recurrent problem with one of the children, an insidious little daydream of success.

In the middle of public worship, we discover ourselves attending not to the hymn we are singing or the sutra the priest is chanting, but to whether the rain will hold off until we have reached home. Or we slip into irritation because the person next to us is singing off-key. We conscientiously force our attention back upon the ultimate or the words in the book of devotion. Our minds drift again. Again compelling ourselves, we focus upon the act of concentration rather than upon the object of our concern. By now the allotted time is up, and we are emptier and more frustrated than when we began.

The first step in the control of wandering thoughts is to expect them. Nearly everyone seems to be afflicted by such vagaries, at least occasionally. Many of us find them a constant hazard. After all, however, our minds are then doing what they were created to do: they are thinking. Let us not discourage them with sharp commands or guilt feelings. Instead, let us turn them gently in the direction we have chosen. Or let us give in to them and go to work on some related aspect of our concern, postponing prayer for the moment while we engage in study or meditation or action. Or let us occupy our minds with a specialized activity appropriate both to the special nature of the mind and to the occasion. This is one of the important functions of a familiar liturgy, especially one that we know by heart: reciting the ritual words, our surface minds are kept busy. If our deeper attention swerves, it meets the ideas expressed in the rite and so is held within the framework of worship.

In a desperate agony of spirit, a man slumps to his knees to beg that he and his beloved may face a disaster with courage. Words break loose from his heart and pour from his lips: "O God, who art the author of peace and lover of concord...." Almost without a pause, "Almighty and most merciful Father, we have erred and strayed from Thy ways like lost sheep...." Then, "Almighty God, unto whom all hearts are open, all desires known, and from whom no secrets are hid, cleanse the thoughts of our hearts...."[5]

What do prayers for peace and purity, and of contrition, have to do with his immediate situation? Conceivably, a connection could be found. Actually, nothing. He is too distraught to search for words that will expresss his terror and his need, yet words he must have to release the thoughts of his heart, words to carry his supplication. *These* words are at hand; he can recite them automatically. They are addressed where he wants them to go, and if with another specific content, what difference does that make? It is not their literal substance that matters. They are trucks carrying the freight of his passion, and any truck will do as long as it is headed in the right direction and is immediately available.

The purpose of a formal rite is to serve as a vehicle for spiritual urgencies. When the rite becomes habitual, it occupies our superficial levels of conscious attention with something that at least approximates our deepest concerns and may embrace them, and so frees us to concentrate upon what matters most to us at that time. Repetition is not in itself vain or empty. Availing ourselves of accustomed movements and memorized words, we do not divide our attention between the substance and the form of our prayer. Because we have mastered the technique, as an expert driver or typist has mastered his machine, we are not diverted from what we are doing by having to figure out how to do it. The familiar words and sounds and gestures become transparent to our intention.

Particular ceremonies and rituals can block or distort worship, either because they are badly constructed or because they do not suit our particular styles. At the time when I am writing this, however, there is a fashion for repudiating the principle of planning worship services, on the ground that improvisation guarantees sincerity. Improvising, however, depends for its success upon skill in that very specialized art, or else on the kind of inspiration that enables a minor poet to write one unforgettable line. The ritual words "I love you" are not necessarily insincere because they are hackneyed. The lover does not repeat them merely because he is expected to, or because he is too stupid to compose another formula. On the contrary, the very strength of his passion compels him to use words that are already heavy with associations and are therefore eminently receptive to the meaning with which he fills them.

No one set of words or gestures or postures is intrinsically superior to others. Yet we need some rituals of standing, sitting, kneeling, lying prostrate, dancing, as well as ritual words, to serve us at those times when we would be distracted by having to select a stance appropriate to our extremity, or when we need the support of habitual ceremony to deliver us from ourselves. As Charles Williams points out, "One of the advantages of ceremony, rightly used, is that it gives a place to self-consciousness, and a means whereby self-consciousness may be lost in the consciousness of the office filled or the ritual carried out".[6]

Ritual is for the worshipper what his craft is to an artist: a skill to be exercised enough that it will be a ready instrument for his inspiration when it comes. It need not be practised at set hours. An established rite for communal worship can be balanced by very flexible forms of private worship. During some periods, it may be desirable to suspend all practice, as an artist may need to lay down his brush or bow or pen for a time of inner regeneration or outer emergency. And the pattern may be highly individual or deeply traditional. But it must not be imposed by force, as in response to an external demand, and it must not be practised simply for the sake of going through the motions.

Engaging in family prayers merely because "the family that prays together, stays together", in the absence of any feeling for an ultimate, represents one kind of forcible imposition. Another is regular attendance at services whose style we are not in sympathy with. Another is rigid persistence in a procedure that once was fruitful but is now barren. Outward forms support the inward spirit; they are not likely to engender it, and there are times when the spirit, being wounded or asleep, should be allowed its periods of seclusion. During such seasons, ritual performance can either serve as a guard over the spirit's rest, or be a vexatious disturbance. Only intuition refined by experience can teach us when the performance of rites will be a sustaining brace, and when a restricting cage.

Ritual and extemporaneous prayer can be useful for either public or private worship, but each requires discipline. In general, group worship is easier if it is planned, so that the worshippers are not distracted by wondering what they should be doing now—and next. Alternatively, it should be led by a person who indicates the steps clearly as he goes along. The exceptions, like the Quaker unprogrammed meeting for worship, depend for their spiritual power upon the presence of individuals who are extremely sensitive to "the leading of the Spirit" not only in themselves but in others, and are highly disciplined in expressing what the Spirit moves them to say. Spontaneity here becomes a sophisticated art of perceiving a situation and responding with exquisitely attuned appropriateness. For some, there is no more intense and exalted mode of corporate worship than this, but it is not suitable for everyone, and it is more easily perverted than any other style of worship I know.

Experiments in adapting the pattern of the "happening" to religious ends display the need for another kind of discipline. The participants are expected to let themselves go, to lose their identity in a communal oneness and express their unity with the ultimate and each other in any behavior which at the moment appeals to them. Often these happenings do not have a formal leader, and they do not always require a common body of beliefs. Doctrine is secondary to "having an experience", and the intellect is deliberately excluded as either unimportant or as evil or to offset what is believed to be an excessive emphasis on doctrine in other communities.

Both the unprogrammed Quaker meeting and the religious happening are far more ceremonial than they appear to be, for the practical reason that unless the group has tacitly agreed upon a framework, too much of its attention has to be spent in deciding on what shall be done and who shall do it. Thus even the agreement that singing, dancing, testifying, preaching, and praying can all be performed simultaneously by different people constitutes a form, and one that makes extreme demands on the individual. At every moment he must choose which of them to do, in what manner, and for how long. The rites of impulsiveness can be glorious fun for a short time, but most of us soon become surfeited with anarchy, and almost despite ourselves develop a formal pattern or turn to the more difficult art of learning to improvise with skill.

Apparently we have more spiritual freedom if we worship together with an accepted design than if we must create a new design at every moment. Only when we are liberated from busyness with form can we fully attend to the meaning it contains and the meaning we bring to it. When we depart from that form on special occasions, we have a base to return to, and when we are ready to change it, we have solid material to work with. The spirit does generate new forms, as well as infuse the old ones with new life, but there is no spiritual benefit in novelty for its own sake—"just to be different".

The use of words and silences to enable prayer and worship is closely related to the use of icons, amulets, music, myths, the prayer shawl, the rosary, the shrine in a corner of the room, the mantra. Like the cellist's bow and the painter's brush, they are tools, but the bow is not suitable for painting on canvas or the paintbrush for playing the cello.

Although icons, myths, music, and so on, can assist us to attain intellectual clarity or to focus our emotions, their primary function is to provide access between the intellect and the imagination. Usually, therefore, we do not deliberately choose which symbol or story shall be for us an image of the ultimate. One or another of them captures us without definable reason. If we start investigating why we are seized by the image of St Christopher, for example, instead of that of St Joseph, it will almost certainly lose its power. As C. S. Lewis warns, "Spiritual experience can never abide introspection"[7]: we learn from such analysis nothing about the spirit, and only a little about the physical and psychological concomitants of spiritual life. Whatever may be appropriate for spiritual masters, we as novices are generally better off if not probing incessantly into our psychological workings. It is one thing to spend our time examining the lenses of our binoculars—symbols and images—and inquiring into the theory of their working. It is something else to look through the binoculars at a bird or a landscape, that is, through the image to what which it images.

Are we refusing tools that are available to us because they are unfashionable—or too fashionable for our tastes? Or because we will not condescend to employ intermediaries like a candle or a sculpture? Or because we do not understand how they work? Are we afraid not only to appear childish, but also to find within our adult selves the primitive child who lives there still?

124

Fear is legitimate; pride is not. And shame is a healthier state than self-deception. Here, the remedy for pride is accuracy in thinking and observing. The remedy for fear is faith—the simple faith that the child in us is also held by the ultimate and will be our friend if we will be friends with it.

As children we had impulses, reactions, tendencies which we have long since put away—or should have. However impatient we may be for Christmas, being adults we take in our stride the necessity to pass through the intervening days before it comes. But have we not discarded other qualities as well, such as imaginative vitality? In our childhood, imagination may have been perilous: confusing dream with reality, we tried to fly like Peter Pan and tumbled from the bed onto the floor. But we learned a wrong lesson from that disaster, to suppress imagination, instead of the fully correct lesson: to balance imagination with reason and vision with fact.

We can achieve balance by diminishing the stronger or by enhancing the weaker—by levelling down or up. Whether intellect or imagination is stronger in us, we must determine for ourselves—or, indeed, whether emotion has buried the two. In making the diagnosis, an experienced spiritual director or soul friend would be of incomparable value, because unless our balance is already reasonably good, we are likely to suppose that we have already approximated what is ideal for us. Or we take for granted that we should work at further strengthening our strengths, and forget about our weaknesses. Or we think that adding more activities to what we are already doing will be sufficient to round out our lives. But the goal is not simply more ingredients; it is their union: to be not just a thinker and, in addition, a lover, but—like Dante—to fuse intellect and passion, body and spirit, into a balanced whole.

Imagination gives us power and material to work with. Intelligence supplies form and control. Imagination alone produces a jungle, intellect alone a desert. Between them, what a grand variety of farms, parks, and gardens: formal, casual, natural, fufilled in a thousand different styles.

All religious rites derive much of their power from their ability to quicken and release those imaginative energies. For the novice, two of the rites are especially important, those of purification and of union. By the essential nature of ritual, they require physical expression. The unity of body and spirit is affirmed in the shaking of the whisk to drive away evil spirits, in speaking aloud the words of confession, in ritual washing. Body-spirit disunity is implied in various ascetical practices designed to subdue the body and distance the world. Although in theory the acts may be no more than physical signs pointing to an inexpressible reality, for the worshiper who is literally or figuratively on his knees, they operate to effectively conjoin all the modes of existence. A movement of the hand in time and space opens a way to that which lies beyond history and matter and full comprehension. The phrases of the prayer reverberate not only from the walls of the room but also from outside the world. Beyond all logic and expectation, the sign communicates the actuality of the thing signified.

Because the function of the rites of purification and union are spiritual and their mode of operation is often imaginative, we cannot measure their efficacy by the intellectual nourishment or emotional excitement which may accompany them. If what we want or expect is a continuation or enhancement of our thoughts and feelings, we may interpret some of our responses to those familiar rites as boredom. But boredom may indicate that we have exhausted the natural resources of the ceremonial words and actions and thus are ready to respond from a different level. What appears to be apathy is sometimes the stilling of the mind and the quieting of the heart which prepare us to receive the spirit, and which we do not recognize because we have not known what to look for or how to judge what comes.

In fairness, it must be added that some religious services are deliberately constructed to be intellectually and emotionally stimulating, with little regard for imaginative or spiritual life. And for circumstances where daily life is normally bleak, those colorful, stirring ceremonies can have great spiritual value. Now and in the West, however, ordinarily we are overstimulated in every way except imaginatively and spiritually, and commonly it is believed that religious institutions must compete with the world and beat it at its own game (which may be an important reason for the current proliferation of new liturgies), instead of providing what the world cannot give: a channel for the cleansing which penetrates to the innermost depth of the self, for the union of the innermost self with the ultimate, and for the uniting of individuals on the deepest level of community.

Only within definite (although not easily definable) limits can we cleanse ourselves spiritually, or achieve spiritual union, in private worship. We are like Frodo, in Tolkien's *The Lord of the Rings*, who at the end cannot take the death-dealing ring from his finger so that it will be destroyed. It must be taken from him. Self-judgement is not, in the long run, enough. Our omissions and transgressions must be judged, and we must be purified, by others or Another, not only because we have offended others, but also because in the end purity is not an achievement but a gift.

Since our direct communion with the ultimate is conveyed through our physical, mental, and psychic apparatus, which are socially grounded, we cannot be corrected and fulfilled except by what reaches us through others. We need somebody else not only to scrub our backs, but also to tell us when our backs need scrubbing. So a spiritual director or soul friend may call our attention to a moral blind spot, or a contradiction between our words and deeds, or a growing impatience or fearfulness or envy that we had not been aware of. Conversely, he may very well attest that we have no warrant for blaming ourselves in certain respects: what we took to be sins were nothing of the kind, and that we can be (are being, have been) cleansed of our real sins. Thereby he supplies us with the resistance and support, freshness and continuity, of a different but compatible viewpoint.

Releasing emotional pressure is not the same as removing whatever impedes our relation to the ultimate, even though psychological factors do, at times, interfere with spiritual development. In theory, psychological counselling and spiritual direction can be performed by a single person who has had dual training, but reorganization and repair, on the one hand, and purification on the other, are no more alike than rearranging the furniture in a house as compared with giving it a thorough house-cleaning. Either operation may lead to the other, or may not, but they call for different skills and produce different results, and neither can adequately substitute for the other. We are dealing here not just with two or more levels of being, but with distinctly diverse functions.

Basically, the rites of purification are not intended to make the participant feel better or function more adequately. Rather, they are like the bath which prepares one for the nuptial union or for surgery, or which washes away the dirt and stains of the day leaving us refreshed for whatever we shall do next. By extension they may serve other functions: in Christianity, for example, the sacrament of confession implies a re-affirmation of the penitent's commitment to God in Christ, and baptism—another purificatory sacrament—involves naming and thereby the affirmation of our identity and place in the world.

The rites of union with the ultimate are also typically communal. Even mystical union, the most intensely private as well as personal religious experience, seems naturally to result in heightened awareness of other people. This may not happen immediately or obviously, and can take a variety of forms, such as increased responsiveness to others and the deepening of intercessory prayer, if not also (as occasionally happens) the exercise of great administrative ability or prophetic leadership. In principle, union with the ultimate excludes nothing. Practically, we may not have the strength to bring into that union more than our individual selves. No matter: let us be content to begin where we are, even though we shall not want to stay there forever. And the formal, public rites provide some of the best means for confirming our direction and increasing our capacity. As before, emotional and intellectual reactions are secondary phenomena, by-products or concomitants, but not measures of the achievement.

Finally, there is the lovely interplay between self-assertion and self-denial, with respect not only to indulgence and asceticism but also to initiating action and waiting for direction, and to giving and receiving. In one of these complementary moves, we affirm our identity as persons and the reality of the world within the ultimate. In the other, we affirm that *sub specie aeternitatis*, we and the world are as nothing. As we choose—or find ourselves driven—to emphasize one or the other, or to hold them counterpoised together, we begin our transition from the ranks of novices and into a field of concentration representing a specific commitment. The period of wide, general exploration and experimentation gives way to a more focussed but also more profound searching. While we are still in our novitiate, however, we shall do well to move freely, and not too solemnly, between activity and passivity, playing with the alternatives and their combinations until we are well acquainted with them.

Denying ourselves things—food, physical comforts, entertainments—is of value in the life of the spirit only to the degree that those particular elements are impediments to wonder and worship. Semi-starvation is usually no better a foundation for spiritual growth than gluttony, even though special types of very advanced discipline require it. For example, Zen Buddhist monks subsist on a diet which is designed to assist meditation by minimizing physical vitality, and as a consequence (I was told by one of them), the occupational disease of those monks is tuberculosis.

The novice has no business even approaching such austerities. Indeed, he must be aware of undertaking, on his own initiative, any serious or prolonged deprivation, lest he use it for the vanity of proving how strong his will has become, or how pure his life. Two kinds of self-denial, however, are relatively safe, and as effective for the beginner as for the experienced. The first is to accept the inevitable losses, disappointments, and mundane distractions of ordinary life as being ascetic disciplines imposed by the ultimate. The second is to rid ourselves of peripheral activities that we do not really, from within ourselves, want to engage in and that are not clearly among our responsibilities. Thus we can offer as a sacrifice the loneliness we are given in place of the fasting we would have willed for ourselves. And we can refuse to interrupt the work we have been called to do, when others are imploring us to serve their particular projects—which may be important and urgent, but are not *ours*.

Neither of these is without its dangers. Is the deprivation, the disappointment, actually inevitable, or are we giving up too soon? Are we really simplifying our lives, or merely constricting them? Are we using our discipline as an excuse to avoid our responsibilities? Doubtless we shall fall into errors of rigidity and laxity, but they are not likely to harm us or anyone else very much unless, stupidly or arrogantly, we go much too far and remain at an extreme for too long. St Teresa of Avila is reputed to have given the excellent advice, "Don't let your sins turn into bad habits". A little common, practical sense, reasonable humility, and the grace to take our enterprise seriously but not with frantic intensity, will markedly reduce the likelihood of permanent damage, even if it does not perfectly protect us from receiving and inflicting minor injury.

Again, a kind of check-list may be of value as a reminder of the many enablements of prayer that are available, each of them attested by one tradition or another, although not all of them (as far as I know) by any single tradition. More or less arbitrarily, I have grouped these enablements as things we perceive and things we do, and I have added one that does not readily fit into either category.

Hearing: The obvious possibilities are sounds (including bells and drums as well as vocal and instrumental music) and silence, but there are more aspects to be taken into account. One of these is the occasional requirement that certain repetitions, as in Christianity of the breviary, be spoken aloud, not just mentally rehearsed, so that not only the mind and voice, but also the ears, are involved. Often the word we hear carries more meaning than the word we only see.

Sight: Yet at the other times, the word we see resonates more strongly than that which we hear. For the most part, however, we associate sight with color as of paintings, stained glass, candle flames; with shapes as of statues, cathedrals, and shrines; and with landscapes, seascapes, and skyscapes with their stars and moon and sun, clouds and lightning. And let us not forget darkness: we bury our face in our hands, our head in our arms, shutting out all visual sensation when it becomes a distraction.

Smell: The burning of incense is customary in many religious traditions, for both public and private worship, and not surprisingly. Fragrances tend to be intensely evocative, summoning memories, invoking moods. The scent of gardenias, of wood-smoke, of baking bread, can lift us out of the immediate into another frame of reference. The Japanese have an incense ceremony which is as attuned to meditation as the tea ceremony, and just as elaborate, although less well known. The sense of smell can be so important to some individuals that they will avoid fragrances even of flowers as tempting them away from their concentration upon the transcendence.

Taste: The wine or grape juice and the bread or wafer of the Christian Eucharist have their counterparts in multifarious ritual meals: the bitter herbs and other elements of the Passover seder, feasts the world over celebrating births, marriages, deaths; and conversely, fasts such as during the Moslem month of Ramadan and the Christian season of Lent.

Touch: Perhaps no other of the senses is as intimately bound up with spirituality as touch. To give only a few examples: the laying-on of hands, the holy kiss, the talisman worn against the skin, the feel of the water in purification ceremonies, the sting of the stick or whip in reproof, the smoothness of the prayer beads slipping between the fingers, the irritation of the hair shirt worn as a penance. Esther Warner describes an incident in which an African gives her "a stone that holds a think". While he tells her what he is thinking, she is to rub the stone with both thumbs and the thought will enter the stone through her thumbs. To recall the thought, she rubs it the same way: "the thought could be summoned into my body through the contact made by my thumbs".[8]

Almost anything we do can be an enablement for spirituality—or (let us not forget) an impediment to it. Some things, however, are especially associated with spirituality and religious observances, such as the following.

Gesture: Crossing oneself or blessing another with the sign of the cross; waving a whisk to purify the immediate area; laying hands on the head or other part of the body; conferring the holy kiss; and other examples under Touch.

Posture: In the West, kneeling for prayer is one of the most common postures, and in the East, the lotus and other yogic positions. But standing, sitting, lying down, prostrating oneself can also be enabling.

Movement: Genuflecting, bowing, pacing the floor, dancing (either performing ritual dances or improvising), walking in a procession, and so on. One of the most important enablements, especially for meditation, is breathing properly, with different ways of breathing prescribed by different traditions, some as simple as "breathe slowly", some as sophisticated as the yogic *pranayama*. Not moving—remaining still—belongs here, too.

Voice: Speaking, singing, shouting, praying aloud, preaching, just talking, keeping silent.

Dress: Putting on a prayer shawl or prayer cap, uncovering the head, removing shoes, wearing vestments or a scapular, "dressing up for church", stripping off all clothing or reducing it to a minimum.

Finally, lighting votive candles, or setting prayer-wheels to turn in flowing water or the wind, have not infrequently been treated as among the sillier of superstitions. As Edmund Crispin has pointed out, however, "Superstition is not mere intellectual error; it is a part of the emotional life, and the worldly-wise who suppress it do so at the risk of impoverishing their souls, an eventuality which for the most part they do not succeed in avoiding".[9] The burning candle or the whirling prayer-wheel confirms by a physical act the nature of the person's concern, that it extends indefinitely beyond the moment when he initiated the act. Thus the objects are invested with a symbolic value that penetrates into the depths beyond conscious awareness. As we go about our other activities, we are united with the significance of the burning candle and the turning wheel as we are united with our dearly beloved during the periods when we are called to exercise our minds upon other matters.

If we were living in a monastic community or hermitage and under a wise spiritual director, we could be bolder in some of our experiments. Most of us, however, have been called to live in a setting which is intrinsically neither more nor less favorable for spiritual life, but which raises different problems and requires different methods—like growing geraniums outdoors instead of in pots on the windowsill. For many centuries and in many places, it was commonly believed that the cloister or hermitage was a necessary condition for spirituality, and in general, the traditional techniques and procedures were developed for that situation. Consequently, we do not have a large and carefully organized reservoir of traditional light to shed on living spiritually within the mundane world, but must grope carefully, as well as bravely, and not burn bridges behind us until we are certain that we shall not want to go back and try a different road.

During our novitiate, the way is broad. It will progressively narrow as we become more sensitive to the ultimate and obey more readily and fully. The first steps toward the life of the spirit are marked by wonder; the first stage consists of that playing around which acquaints us with the spiritual domain and with our own inclinations and potentialities. The moment of passing from interest to commitment may or may not be marked by a conscious rite of passage. Often, we realize only long after the event that that change has taken place. Even then, we shall continually be discovering uncommitted areas and undeveloped capacities in ourselves, and must return sometimes to intellectual or emotional or spiritual primers although most of the rest of our life is being lived on the graduate or even the professional level.

CHAPTER SIX

Impediments to Prayer

Every mystical writing that I have ever seen tells, in effect, the same story—not that the man attained to God but that he was at last able to overcome his carnal and intellectual resistance to God.

Charles Morgan
Reflections in a Mirror,
Second Series, 83

Whatever may have been true in other periods and may be true now in other places, one of the most serious impediments to spiritual life today in the West is the identification of emotional excitement with spiritual vitality. Because ecstatic states sometimes (not always, by any means) accompany and sometimes follow a confrontation with the ultimate, we tend to conclude—mistakenly—that if only we can achieve

137

ecstasy, we shall have life in the spirit. A side-effect is taken as a means to the end, or worse, as itself the end. Sensational shocks are substituted for deeply perceptive awareness, and the paralysis of concussion for the stillness of wonder.

Currently, therefore, those who hunger for spiritual sustenance are easily misled into supposing that all ecstasies are revelations from or of the ultimate, and if their desire grows fierce enough, they will go to almost any lengths in order to evoke a "religious experience". They seize as a right what is meant as a gift, and so forfeit the blessing that accompanies the gift. Manipulating their bodies with drugs, stupefying their minds with noise, hardening their hearts against others, inevitably they remain still unsatisfied, and so press on toward even more violent experiences.

Approaching from another direction are those who are convinced that worship can be renewed by liturgies designed to stimulate the intellect, arouse the emotions, or spur congregations into immediate action, thereby raising still higher the barriers against receptivity, contemplation, and wonder. The essential processes of spiritual growth are traded for a program which differs only superficially from the entertainment and instruction available from myriads of mundane sources.

Medical and psychological management have reached the stage where they can give us almost any experience we please, and enable us to impose on others almost any state of consciousness or set of propositions. Brainwashing makes it possible to destroy the person who informs the body. Psychotherapy can help to disburden us of hindrances to healthy personal growth. But none of these means can compel the action of the ultimate upon us, or our response to the ultimate. Psychedelic drugs can intensify sensation and emotion to an intolerable pitch, carrying us far out of ourselves into an experience which is indistinguishable *as an experience* from the mystical encounter. But the heart of the mystical vision is not the experience of ineffable sights and sounds or the incommunicable emotions, but the nature of that which is encountered, and which pierces and purifies and integrates.

The encounter with the ultimate verifies the experience; the experience does not verify the encounter, because emotions, sensations, and ideas can be produced by a great many natural agencies. Moreover, authentic spiritual encounter can be accompanied by a very wide range of emotions other than ecstasy; to give only a few examples: shame, gratitude, adoration, fear, tranquility, amazement, dread, and laughter as well as tears.

How, then, should the spiritual novice use psychedelic or tranquilizing drugs, electrical stimuli to pleasure-centers in the brain, surgical disruption of anxiety centers, and so on? Only with the clear knowledge that they are impediments to *spiritual* life. Biologically, intellectually, and emotionally they may have positive value in certain exigencies.

As for the less potent drugs, from aspirin to alcohol, if we had begun our novitiate in childhood, we might as adults be strong and skilled enough to live spiritually without such crutches, within the over-crowded, over-stimulating conditions of modern civilization. As it is, there may be occasions when it is all we can do to keep functioning in a way that is endurable to ourselves and others. Tranquilizers, soporifics, and analgesics can provide us with brief "vacations" to save us from prostration. Far better than a capsule would be a weekend away from home and business, a day at a retreat house, an evening at a concert or play. But we cannot always afford them, even if we could find a quiet place to travel to, a center for prayer, or the type and quality of music that would restore us.

Refusing temporary palliatives is a form of asceticism, and we gain nothing spiritually by undertaking ascetic practices before we are ready for them. Conversely, there is no spiritual advantage in running to the pill-bottle at every twinge of discomfort. If all life is to be brought at last under the aspect of eternity, we must bring under it as much of our strains and frustrations as we are able to endure without critically slighting our responsibilities. The impulse to take drugs may indicate that some of the duties we have taken upon ourselves are not in fact necessary for us to do. The symptoms may be a call to divest ourselves of extrinsic occupations, and masking the symptoms with drugs can prevent an accurate diagnosis and appropriate corrective measures. Or the symptoms may indicate a physiological imbalance which ought to be corrected by medical means, if any are available.

As we stand between the perils of self-indulgence and self-punishment, between weakly pampering and harshly manhandling ourselves, the worst danger lies not in making a mistake every now and then, but in clinging to either extreme. When we are able to recognize our mistakes, and are willing to learn from them, we need only to be careful, not timid.

One who is in earnest about the life of the spirit almost certainly will leave the so-called mind-expanding preparations alone, unless under the direction of those trained in a religious tradition that requires them and safeguards their use, as do some Native American religions with peyote. Surely we can trust the ultimate to expand our minds at the time and to the degree that is right for us, without recourse to external aids.

Whether in plants, animals, or human beings, health depends upon proportion. However common the spindly intellectual and the mindless athlete may be in fiction, they are relatively rare in fact. But the one-track-minded sensationalists seem to be growing in numbers and influence. Immolating their minds and repudiating their social obligations, they are already numerous enough to jeopardize those who are striving toward wholeness and holiness. The method of simplifying by exclusion is immensely appealing because it is easier to live with only one part of oneself than to articulate many elements and functions into a smoothly-running, coherent entity, but such superficial ease is not a way toward the ultimate.

Behind the stolid or severe or affable faces we present to the world, many of us conceal more emotional stresses than we are able to handle constructively, so we bind them in chains for fear of their destructive potentialities. Until we have raised our minds and spirits to an equivalent strength, we dare not relax our self-restraint. Our goal, however, is neither to conquer passion nor surrender to it, but to join it in a merry dance—we who as yet can scarcely stand on our feet or catch the intricate rhythm of the celestial music.

There is nothing inherently damaging to spiritual life in the pinnacles of emotion and sensation, any more than the thin air of the high mountains is inherently damaging to the normally healthy body. Unless one is acclimated, however, the peaks can kill. Jeremy Taylor warns, "Let no man be hasty to eat of the fruits of Paradise before his time",[1] and the prophet Isaiah, "He that believeth shall not make haste",[2] and Teresa of Avila, "Many souls ... want to fly before God gives them wings".[3]

Although in our day probably the most critical impediment to spiritual life is mistaking exalted experience for encounter with the ultimate, I suspect that the most widespread impediment is the inner confusion or impurity or resistance that hinders us from receiving the ultimate fully and freely. Something within our nature as persons opposes the invasion of the transcendent Other, and indeed, often of mundane others. No two cultures or religions are likely to agree in detail on what this something is and how it is to be identified and dealt with. But all, or nearly all, religions provide rites of purification that some anthropologists[4] interpret as being at once positive means for affirming and restoring personal and social order, and negative rejections of disorder. Such rites reflect our awareness that we are not worthy to receive the vision, and our observation that when it comes, we are abashed by our unworthiness.

To feel no need for purification or enlargement is a symptom of spiritual immaturity or senility. To be paralyzed with guilt is a symptom of spiritual disease. Within those limits, the discovery of what acts or states inhibit our receiving the ultimate must be directed by experience—experience gained both by our observing from the outside and by participating from within.

The history and traditions of mankind are replete with commandments and prohibitions that can be immeasurably valuable as suggestions, even when we do not take them as prescriptions. Some ethical codes and rules of courtesy, for example, look as if they were more directly concerned with fostering purity of heart than with establishing stable social organizations. Thus behind the various caste systems may lie the conviction that it is essential for spiritual life to give our fellows the respect and concern which is their due—a principle that can well be defended even when we disagree on what is indeed due to any given person, and why it is due to him. The heavy talk about sins may reflect immemorial knowledge of human imperfection, penetrating deeper than the neat categories of our social and behavioral sciences. In looking into such matters, it is a waste of time to start over from scratch, without reference to the wisdom of our predecessors. Why should we repeat their errors, retrace their footsteps down all the dead ends and into all the deadly by-ways? We may dislike their langauge. We may decry their forms of expression. But the doctrines of impurity and sin speak of, and to, a most fundamental human experience of inadequacy. To quote G. K. Chesterton:

> Modern masters of science are much
> impressed with the need of beginning all
> inquiry with a fact. The ancient masters of
> religion were quite equally impressed with
> that necessity. They began with the fact of
> sin—a fact as practical as potatoes. Whether
> or no man could be washed in miraculous
> waters, there was no doubt at any rate that

143

he wanted washing. But certain religious
leaders . . . have begun in our day not to deny
the highly disputable water, but to deny the
indisputable dirt.[5]

It would be tempting to embark on research to identify the causes of our inadequacy, in the hope of erad-
icating our uncleanness or eliminating our inner
restrictions in one great, if painful, operation. Should
we not pull up the weeds by their roots, not merely
cut them back? Yes—if we could be sure of differentiating weeds from valuable plants that need only
to be pruned or moved to another place, and if, in any
case, this is a task we are competent to perform.

The novice clearly is not ready for such drastic action. He is too likely to be guided by those around
him who are diagnosing healthy growth of individuality as selfishness, rightful obedience as irresponsibility, and worship as escapism. Nowhere is our sense
of inadequacy more compelling than in our willingness
to accept the worst possible constructions of our own
motives and behavior. In our novitiate, therefore, we
can and probably should defer theoretical investiga-
tions into the sources of human resistance in favor of
a different kind of work. "It is one thing, and no doubt
a proud and subtle thing, to repel philosophical error;
it is another, and a simpler, to say, Get thee behind
me, Satan".[6]

Our Satan is the actual way in which at *this* moment
we are resisting the ultimate. Busyness or laziness?
Pride or false shame? Ignorance or guilt? Irritation or
cynicism? Depression or manic fervor? Direct attack
upon those demons is one way to repel them, although
usually not the best way. The conquest of sloth, for

example, by determinedly saying to our selves, "Go to, now, work!" is likely to be less effective than finding an activity, be it painting, gardening, or making clothes, which is so exciting, so satisfying, that we become energetic in order to free enough time to do it.

Some hindrances can be circumvented: an unpleasant or boring routine like washing dishes, now an occasion for resentment, can give the opportunity we have been seeking for regular, solitary prayer or meditation, or memorizing poetry, or working out a problem. One of our sharpest weapons is the twist of mental perspective that reveals how funny we are and provokes us to laughter—not the forced, painful laughter of "I shouldn't take myself so seriously", but the happy laughter of realizing all over again that we are neither fiends nor holy angels, but human beings.

Most if not all traditions specify certain behaviors and attitudes as sins, which is to say, offences against the ultimate and impediments to spirituality. For convenience, here I shall list only those which Christianity has specified as being "deadly" or "mortal" sins, so called because persistence in them leads to spiritual death. My description of these depends heavily on Dorothy L. Sayers' lecture "The Other Six Deadly Sins",[7] and her Notes on Dante's "Purgatory".

1. The root sin, from which all the others derive, is *pride*—not so much arrogance or conceit as what the Greeks meant by *hubris*, the sin of trying to be gods or, alternatively, of trying to use a god as an instrument for our own purposes, of seeing ourselves to be not in a second place absolutely. It is the sin to which the pious, the idealist, and the moralist are most sus-

ceptible, often revealing itself in the "holier than thou" attitude or the claim to be "master of my fate and captain of my soul".

2. Dorothy L. Sayers describes *envy* as "the sin of the Have-Nots against the Haves".[8] How often have we heard—and said—in effect, "If I can't have it, you shouldn't either", whether it be wealth or intelligence or skill? Miss Sayers says more specifically,

> In love, Envy is cruel, jealous, and possessive. My friend and my married partner must be wholly wrapped up in me, and must find no interests outside me. That is my right. No person, no work, no hobby must rob me of any part of that right. If we cannot be happy together, we will be unhappy together—but there must be no escape into pleasures that I cannot share.[9]

3. In contrast, *avarice* is "the sin of the Haves against the Have-Nots",[10] the coveting of material possessions for their own sake, or for the power bestowed by wealth. It can be manifested in miserliness or conspicuous consumption, or in overwhelming ambition for high place and great power.

These three—pride, envy, and avarice—are sins of the cold heart and the calculating mind, of those whose lives are concentrated upon manipulating the world for their own benefit.

4. Between the cold- and the warm-hearted sins lies *sloth*, which is much more than mere laziness. It is characterized by "the empty heart and the empty brain",[11] and Miss Sayers writes of it:

146

One form of it which appeals very strongly to some modern minds is that acquiescence in evil and error which readily disguises itself as "Tolerance"; another is that refusal to be moved by the contemplation of the good and beautiful which is known as "Disillusionment," and sometimes as "knowledge of the world"; yet another is that withdrawal into an "ivory tower" of Isolation which is the peculiar temptation of the artist and the contemplative, and is popularly called "Escapism". [12]

The warm-hearted and hot-headed sins are wrath, gluttony, and lust, all of which are perversions of virtues.

5. *Wrath* is righteous indignation carried to the extreme of rage "without restraint and without magnanimity". [13]

6. The satisfaction of hunger is one thing. It is another thing, the sin of *gluttony*, to over-indulge in food or drink, or to be excessively finical in what one eats or drinks. By extension, the gluttonous include those for whom bodily comfort is a primary goal.

7. Finally, *lust* is desire, sexual or other, divorced from love, affection, caring, personal concern for another or others.

Sins can be committed unwittingly, in ignorance that they are sins. Or sins can be committed deliberately. Or they can be mistakenly attributed, as when we are accused of apathy when we are simply—and perhaps intensely—interested in something other than what our accuser wants us to be interested in. Tireless ambition, to the point of grinding others under one's heel, has been considered a virtue by some—take Scrooge, for example, before the Christmas ghosts persuaded him otherwise, or for another example, the parents who, having been battered in their childhood, consider it right and proper to batter their children. Or those who know with both their heads and hearts that it is wrong to kill, but in an access of fury do kill. Or those who carefully plan to destroy a competitor in business or love, rationalizing their action as "self-defense".

To speak of sins is one thing, and there is value in self-examination to identify the particular ways in which we are sinning. It is another thing to think of sins not one by one but "like a lump",[14] as the author of *The Cloud of Unknowing* advises in distinguishing between committing particular sins and being sinful.

What differentiates sin from other transgressions is that they are presumed to be violations not of arbitrary enactments, but of the very principles by which the universe is ordered. Sins are to be compared not with the laws regulating traffic, but with the laws of gravitation and thermodynamics. We do not break the laws of physics or of our fundamental relationships with the universe. They break us if we contravene them. The penalty—which is not punishment but inevitable consequence—may not be imposed on the spot, but it is none the less sure. It may or may not be true, as the cynic claims, that virtue is its own reward, but indubitably the wages of sin is death in one form or another, unless a right relationship with the ultimate is restored.

Many of the obstacles to the life of the spirit issue from the world around us: incessant noise; pervasive ugliness; lack of food or too much of it; too little or too much comfort; most of all, the dominant mood of our time and place, whether God- or man-centered, rational or devotional, voluptuous or austere. A society which takes religious organizations, doctrines, and practices as normative can be as hampering to spiritual life as a vehemently anti-religious society. The one makes spirituality too easy and external; the other makes it too difficult and inward. The remedy, however, is neither social revolution nor—for most of us—the establishment of pilot projects in spiritual community, or admission to a religious order. Without for a moment impugning the eternal value of natural goodness, the fact remains that invariably the spirit stands in contrast or in opposition to the mundane world. Either contrast or opposition may constitute a judgement that ultimately natural and social perfection are not good enough, or they are not complete in themselves.

To say that the world is the enemy of the spirit does not necessarily mean that the mundane world is evil, or is too gross to unite with the spirit. It may mean instead that the mundane is as yet too immature to receive the impregnation of the spirit, or only is not—as the world commonly claims to be—sufficient unto itself and self-perfecting. Our turning away from the world may represent not a refusal of its demands and our responsibilities, but the affirmation that it and we together are subject to an authority transcending us both. Francis of Assisi, rejecting the lordship of the world, re-entered it as the world's companion in joy and misery, patient endurance and prophetic fire.

According to the evidence from many religious traditions, we who are on the way of the spirit must in some sense abandon the world in order to achieve the perspective that will enable us to live creatively within it. All the traditions that I am familiar with, however, allow considerable freedom for the individual to choose what form his abandonment will take, from becoming a hermit to remaining with his family and continuing his customary occupations while centering his life on the ultimate. He can give the world as much of his love and labor as he chooses, short of his *ultimate* devotion and obedience.

During the early, exploratory period which I am calling our novitiate, we learn whether we are prepared to renounce the world as our ultimate authority. If we choose to remain worldly, neither false pride nor false humility should deter us. Although probably life in the spirit is open to anyone who is capable of being surprised, we may not be ready now to direct our entire lives to the source of wonder. This may not be the right time for us. And "He who professes only nature may be rewarded with the best of nature, perhaps with more than nature; he who professes more than nature, if he does not practise it, may be left with neither".[15]

It has sometimes been said that the life of the spirit is the highest attainable by persons, but those who make that claim are likely to be the first to warn of its dangers. Denying the world's supremacy and finality, we invite its resentment. Affirming the spirit, we become vulnerable to attacks and infiltrations from within the complex domain of the spiritual, which includes not only "divine" but also "demonic" powers, and we know very little about either. The end of natural and social life, presumably, is compassionate death, but for spiritual life, there is said to be no end or respite or escape.

150

How far we shall finally be called to go in adopting an extraordinary mode of life, we cannot know in advance. I suspect that for most of us, the change will lie primarily in the significance of what we do rather than in altered behaviors. The ultimate will impregnate our nature, not lead us to forsake nature. If we are concerned to hear and obey the present word that is spoken to us, we need not concern ourselves overmuch with the future.

Reasonable prudence with respect to natural situations is certainly called for, but there is no need to anticipate titanic spiritual battles, public martyrdom, or any other such dramatic episodes, as consequences of the decision to live *sub specie aeternitatis*. As Charles Williams says, the practice of all religions "is, frequently, almost unmitigated boredom or even a slow misery, in which the command to rejoice always is the most difficult of all".[16] And because the ultimate is timeless, our spiritual future does not matter, nor our spiritual past, but only the present in which we listen or close our ears, obey or disobey.

Yet at the same time that we live under the aspect of eternity, we live also in history where past, present, and future do matter. Here, in another form, we have the contrast or opposition between the transcendental and the mundane, which may represent enmity or judgement, or a potentially joyous contrast, or a combination of these and other relationships.

An important corollary to this view of the relation of spirit and world is that we can begin the life of the spirit within any outward circumstances whatever. Many spiritual leaders of the past, including the Buddha and St Paul, have been accused of tolerating or approving such institutions as slavery and economic injustice, when their intention, it seems, was only to say, in effect, "Even though all other good things are forcibly withheld from you, the highest good, the supreme joy, is already within your reach. It is yours for the asking, now". That teaching neither justifies nor condemns social structures, but provides an immediate answer to the urgent, immediate problem, "How can I live at all, *now*?"

From the very beginning when we first felt the stillness of wonder laid like a hand upon us, our worship has almost certainly been impeded by intellectual questions and ethical dilemmas. "What—or whom—am I praying to? Am I on the right way? Why is this happening? How can I find out?" The nature of language and of analytical thought has required us to postpone our talk about intellect and morality, but experience is more complex. All the while, our intellectual experience has twined and intertwined with our worship so intricately that in following the strand of worship, we may have lost our appreciation for the other elements in the pattern. The necessary analysis is only a prelude to synthesis, but before we can synthesize overtly and in good earnest, we must take up some of the ways in which the intellect itself can temporarily limit or permanently block our access to the ultimate.

Almost inevitably, we approach the ultimate expecting from it too much or too little or the wrong things—perhaps an instant and violent transformation, or a gentle confirmation of our way of life, or a substitute for vigorous intellectual work or physical activity. Being prepared to see the light of a countenance, so to speak, we do not notice the touch of a hand. Our anticipations can be so strong that they constitute, in effect, demands. For example, we may refuse to worship until all our rational problems have been solved, or all our emotional or physical wants have been supplied. How *can* we pray when our bellies are clamoring for food, our lover has left us, our logical categories have been outraged? Yet we must.

If we insist on having a heaven on earth and within ourselves before we can look beyond the earth and become new selves, we are spiritually dead before we ever came alive. As far as I know, none of the founders of a major religion has taught that natural fulfilment is a precondition for spiritual achievement. On the contrary, openly or implicitly they have said that without the spirit, our minds and hearts will never be satisfied, our bodies—although sated—will never be content, and our societies may be organized but will never be communities.

Neither intellectual clarity nor moral purity is necessary for worship. On the other hand, without intellectual probing and moral effort, worship is stringently limited. Intellectual investigation, however, depends in part upon intellectual freedom and scope, qualities that today are not in abundant supply. For all the talk about liberating the mind, too often the form in which it appears is the liberty to shout obscenities, or to propagate verbal unclarity and intellectual confusion. How many now are learning to enter the thought-forms of the past or of other cultures, so as to release themselves from their bondage to the present moment and place? That is a freedom worth having, even at the price of being laughed at or ignored. Moreover, it is a freedom vital for spiritual growth, because the ultimate is not confined to a single period of history or geographical area. Much less is it accessible through annual fashions.

It is hard to overestimate the pressures which currently bear upon those who are trying to live in a house larger than the cells chosen by many of their contemporaries, or even merely to equip their cells with dignified and beautiful furnishings. The badge of nonconformity is flourished by groups who maintain within their own ranks an inflexible conformity. Daily we read or hear the results of public-opinion polls informing us of where we stand in a classification whose divisions we have no possibility of overriding. At best, we are identified as "other". The books in our stores and libraries, the classes in our schools, are chosen with a keen eye to general appeal. Because only these are widely available, general appeal swiftly proceeds toward universal adoption. With regard to television, a commentary written some years ago by Charles Morgan about movies is *a fortiori* applicable to the TV screen. Morgan admits, to begin with, the liberating, entertaining, and informing values of certain films, and then goes on to say:

> The damage is done by averaging and habit. . . . The evil of its regular use is much less in the corruptive energy of particular exhibitions of violence than in the films' collective, habit-making power to satisfy imaginative hunger "out of a can" and so to discourage the secret, individual imagination from following its own quarry. . . . [For a viewer] to be told by the sound-track what the damsel played on her dulcimer and to see the milk of paradise poured from a jug is a suicide

of part of himself. It is, precisely, the form of suicide that the Litany prays against—a hardening of heart, a contempt of the Word— which by possessing the mind with a false image, excludes truth. It is a submission to the powers of evil, which seek to debase the currency of imagination wherever they find it.[17]

By such pervasive means, we are encouraged to think others' thoughts and see others' visions, rather than to think with our own minds, see with our own eyes, and dream our own dreams. It is not surprising, therefore, that sooner or later we confront an "identity crisis" and blindly resort to such cheap expedients as basing our personal identity on impersonal categories like color, sex, or political party. History and legend, and those works of imagination which deal at once severely and compassionately with human life, would have taught us that personal identity does not arise out of identification with mass movements. We are saved or damned not by what but by who we are.

Often, I suspect, we seek identity in "what" rather than "who" because we have not studied the alternatives exhibited in history, literature, and so on, and are not inventive enough to rediscover them by ourselves. "Few ideas of virtue remain but those which arise from civic conformity, and little understanding that any other notion of virtue has prevailed among men".[18] Always, however, we bear at least a shred of responsibility for our ignorance. We could have followed up this hint from our reading, that example in our neighbor, of a life not bounded by "averaging and habit", and a mind not coerced by others' opinions.

155

The life of the spirit does not require intellectual brilliance, but we can use all the intelligence we have, plus some degree of intellectual independence in the willingness—and the courage—to think for ourselves, if only by accepting our responsibility to decide which among all the competing authorities we shall defer to.

A particular form of intellectual hindrance to spiritual life is generated by the failure to discriminate between spirituality, the psychic, and witchcraft. In principle, psychic abilities such as telepathy, extrasensory perception, and clairvoyance are no more mysterious than artistic or mathematical abilities, and no more evenly distributed among persons. Taken as a behavioral rather than as a quasi-physical phenomenon, a psychic event is as intelligible as any other instance where the exercise of an ability leads to an achievement. In principle, therefore, spirituality and the psychic have no difficulty in coming to terms.

Sorcery or witchcraft, however, is a different matter. The sorcerer claims access to and control within a domain that is neither mundane nor holy and that—unlike the mundane and the spiritual worlds—is open only to those who have been initiated by esoteric rites. That domain is characterized by a system of fundamental concepts and logical relationships that constitutes an alternative to our mundane and scientific views of the world, as well as to spirituality—this last, because sorcery is in essence manipulative.

As an alternative to spirituality, sorcery is appealing on several counts, among them that it is exotic; that it is promoted by a tightly knit, exclusive community; and that it promises almost limitless power. It shares these attractions with other social entities, of course—

certain religious or pseudo-religious cults, for example. But the kind and degree of power which the sorcerer professes to wield is in a class by itself, and whether that power be used for good or evil is less important than his intention to coerce persons and states of affairs in accordance with his will.

But do not all of us use coercion upon occasion? Yes, but we do not call upon superhuman and supernatural forces to implement our desires—and at this point, the issue is not whether such forces exist and, if they do, whether they can be manipulated by the sorcerer. At issue is the sorcerer's claims and methods, which are diametrically opposed to what is claimed for spirituality.[19]

The proper use of power—intellectual, emotional, social, physical, spiritual, and any other—is itself a spiritual, as well as a practical and ethical, problem. There can be no doubt but that power tends to corrupt; equally, however, powerlessness tends to corrupt. The ultimate does not call us to be inactive, and to be active involves our using whatever powers we have. We are to be neither "early Christian doormats" nor monarchs of all we survey. Especially, the ultimate is not subject to our control, and sooner or later it retaliates decisively upon those who are bent upon an ultimate mastery.

We can deny or defy the essential nature of things, but only a person who is mad with hubris can believe he has any possibility of succeeding, or if he tries to do so, of escaping a destruction as entire as his insolence. Indeed any of us can slip into such an attitude occasionally, then seeing what we have done, reject that tendency and turn back from the pretension that we are gods to the clear knowledge that we are human.

The infinite penalty is not assessed upon a momentary lapse. Even a flicker of such an inclination, however, is perilous, although the novice—perhaps—will be less inclined to such delusions of grandeur than the adept.

Traditions differ on whether the body as such is a hindrance or a help to spirituality. They appear to agree, however, that it cannot be ignored or treated as negligible. There are two principal schools of thought: either spirit is unhappily confined in our physical flesh, or the flesh is a vehicle for spiritual life—"the spirit waiting for the letter, without which it cannot perfectly be".[20]

Most if not all traditions agree on the need for physical disciplines. These can range from regular periods of fasting or a limited diet to flagellation, and from life-long celibacy to the kind of physical exercise that goes with keeping house or walking to work or farming or dancing. What form the discipline of the body takes seems to be less important than having *some* discipline, *some* rule of life, rigid or flexible, and not only designed for the specific tradition but also adapted for the specific individual.

Here again we need to remember that what is an impediment for one person can be an enablement for another, and that these early stages are times for experimenting to find which way is the best for us. Our bodily rhythms do make a difference: for example, apparently some of us are born larks, at our best in the day, and others born nightingales. C. S. Lewis considers bedtime to be the worst time of all for concentrated prayer;[21] for Gerald Heard, then and during the night is the best.[22] There may be virtue in com-

pelling ourselves to pray, against our natural procliv-
ities, at dawn or midnight, but common sense suggests
that until we are well established in prayer, we do it
at the times when we are naturally most open and
aware.

To take another example, rituals such as the Native
American vision quest, which call for refraining from
all food for several days, would be devastating and
possibly fatal for a diabetic or hypoglycemic. Ill health
can compound our spiritual difficulties, the malaise of
the body affecting our spiritual vitality. We may chide
ourselves, "I *ought* to be able to rise above this", to
which the only adequate response would be, "Why?"
It requires years of rigorous training to run a four-
minute mile or to become an Olympic-caliber fencer;
why do we expect of ourselves, as novice spiritual
athletes, a comparable proficiency? Indeed we can and
should try either to rise above our afflictions or to carry
them into the transcendent, but there should be no
shame if we fail. Now we can go only so far; later we
can go farther. And for some the achievement comes
more easily than for others. Let us not, however, pretend to ourselves that our ailments are "a means of
grace" if in fact they are not.

How we bring our bodies into collaboration with
our spiritual development depends in part upon our
physical equipment, in part upon how we envision
the relationship between the physical and the spiritual
domains. Or to state the problem in another way: what
kind of beings must we become if we are to live most
fully under the aspect of eternity? Disembodied spirits
or embodied persons? Are our bodies to be cast aside
or transformed? Does nature have a place within the
ultimate, or is it excluded? If we follow the principle

that we cannot give what we do not have, presumably the novice should not begin by seeking release from his body. On the opposite principle that the body is an entanglement, he should free himself from it as rapidly and as thoroughly as possible. The goal is the same in both cases, however: life under the aspect of eternity. The diversity of methods reflects the diversity of individuals, and of their circumstances, histories, and world views.

One particularly valuable way to come to terms with the relation of our bodies to the ultimate is by meditating upon our approaching death—because whatever our age and physical condition, we are approaching that culmination. Usually such meditation does not focus upon what comes after death, but rather upon the letting-go itself. We have all had some practice in dying, as we have gone through little deaths of moving from one neighborhood or school to another, losing familiar people and places and habitual ways of doing ordinary things. We have to let our children go as they grow up and leave our homes; let go relatives, friends, and heroes when they die; let go our childhood, youth, maturity.

But to let go the very eyes we see the world with, the ears we hear its sounds with, the hands with which we touch it, and for all we know, the minds with which we think and the hearts with which we love … to let the world go: winds, dandelions, street crowds, traffic lights, autumn colors, all the dear familiarity of living, to let them all go: that is different. We may be convinced that after death we shall see with better eyes and hear with better ears, and that our imperfect bodies will be changed into perfect ones. In agony, we

160

may pray for death. All the same, the loss is real and piercing.

Facing death, we face implacably our responsibility for our lives, for being who we are. We can no longer excuse ourselves on the ground that we were following a prophet, a teacher, a book, a spiritual guide, a vision, because it was we who gave them the status of "authority". Neither can we excuse ourselves on the ground that we did not listen to those prophets, teachers, and so on, because there were many times when we knew that we should have heeded them. Not having an authority can be as severe an impediment as having one. Then there were the restraints we placed on ourselves: "I'm too stupid to—" ... "I'm a man, therefore I must—" ... "As a woman and wife, I cannot—" ... "I have committed this sin, therefore—" ... "Having given up that, I deserve—". At death, we are left with nothing but ourselves, whatever we may be, and with the ultimate, whatever that may be.

To anticipate in meditation that definitive stripping can be as disturbing as the prospect of leaving behind all that we have when we flee a fire or flood, or as refreshing as looking forward to casting off our winter clothes on the first warm day in spring. Either way, the purpose of the exercise is the same: not so much to prepare ourselves for dying (although that does have its place) as to make us aware of the form that our lives are taking, the form that is completing itself in us.

"The chief difficulty of living", writes Charles Morgan, "is the difficulty we all have in perceiving what the form of our life really is or indeed that it has a form".[23] In meditating upon our own deaths, we can

161

begin to discern the form that we have created hitherto, and how it can be brought more nearly into conformity with what we are called to be. How we are bringing it into conformity is not, fundamentally, a matter of wresting ourselves to be what we are not, because—again quoting Morgan—"The freedoms of the spirit are not attained by violence of the will but by an infinite patience of the imagination".[24]

Late in the sixteenth century, when St John of the Cross described the Dark Night of the Soul, apparently he was spared one of its most debilitating features: the uncertainty whether this was veritably a spiritual visitation to be endured with patient submission to the will of God, or a psychological depression to be treated by any of a number of therapies. It is a question that we in the twentieth century cannot avoid with respect to our whole spiritual lives.

The reductionist gambit by which spiritual phenomena are dismissed as "merely psychological" is employed against us not only by cynics but also by ourselves. Beyond question, psychological states affect our spiritual states, and vice versa, but the relations between them are not so simple that psychological health will ensure spiritual growth, or that spiritual resources can be depended upon to correct psychological aberrations. Not all depressions are Dark Nights, by any means; neither does every spiritual block reflect a psychological disorder. How can we tell which is which?

I do not know of any way to tell. All I can offer is the Quaker rule of thumb, "Proceed as the way opens". Here, yet again, we must experiment, remembering that the ultimate is not impotent or inactive. We need to remember as well that we are not a combination of psychological and spiritual elements, but integral persons with many functions and aspects. It is possible, therefore, in many cases to deal with situations integrally, not differentiating the psychological and the spiritual dimensions. Two illustrations may help to clarify what this means. The first comes from Charles Morgan, who tells of a nun who was vowed to the care of children of the very poor, but was so obsessed by the desire for travel that it threatened not only her vocation but her stability. He writes:

> The remedy she . . . discovered was as strange as the desire itself. Whenever the longing to travel came upon her, and unknown rivers and mountains and cities would not be banished from her thoughts and dreams, by a single act of acceptance she converted prospect into retrospect, and said: "I have come home from a long journey", and went among her children that day in the mood of one who had been long absent, seeing them afresh, loving them afresh, perceiving them with new, unstaled recognitions.[25]

The second illustration comes from a friend of mine who was profoundly angered and embittered at an injustice against himself, to the point where he could neither work nor rest in peace. He could not, in conscience, pray for the perpetrators' destruction, and his prayers for deliverance from "being imprisoned by these ugly emotions" did not release him. After a long time it occurred to him that—to use his figure of speech—Screwtape (C. S. Lewis' demonic letter-writer)[26] and his minions were using the perpetrators as a means to ravage him. He took to reading the Psalms promising that evildoers shall be cut off and our enemies be made our footstool, directing his rage for destruction against the satanic powers that were acting through the human perpetrators. In good conscience he could, and did, pray most fervently that "Screwtape" would be destroyed. His release did not come immediately but in fits and starts, yet it did come, by the process that Morgan describes as "rather in passing through an impediment than in resisting an assault".[27]

The transformation of an impediment into an enablement is seldom simple or easy—read, for example, the record of St John's suffering through the Dark Night. Nearly all the writers of spiritual classics which I have read (but I am not a scholar in the field) minimize their excursions into byways and dead ends, except as they label them—after the fact—"temptations". Thereby the authors convey the impression that they had no real difficulty in finding their way once they started on it. For the most part, however, they are looking back and therefore can see the pattern clearly, which is small comfort and smaller guidance for those of us who are looking forward, often with no ready-made signposts to warn us away from taking roads that would be unprofitable for us. Let us listen carefully to our predecessors, however, when from their vantage point at the end of the road, they proclaim with a single voice that the game is more than worth the candle.

PART THREE

Life in the Spirit

Interior discipline is only a preparing of the ground
. . . what makes the ground fruitful comes, like
seed and rain and sun, from outside oneself.
Philosophy is the female aspect of the contemplative
act. Visitation is necessary, and whoever has been
made aware of the possibility of it waits for it
always; his life has no other continuous meaning or
purpose.

Charles Morgan
Sparkenbroke, 385

CHAPTER SEVEN

The Life of the Mind

So with the great poets; where they adored, they defined.

Charles Williams
"Il ben dell' Intelletto"

Inevitably, we begin our conscious, deliberate life in the spirit with a theology of sorts, a more or less explicit set of concepts and expectations, beliefs and doubts, which we have picked up from many sources, organized casually, and rarely questioned except when we were directly challenged by some critical incident or cynical friend.

Almost from the air around us, we have absorbed a

167

climate of opinion that modifies the weather of our thinking. "Of course the world is (or is not) inhabited by kami ... spirits ... ghosts ... the souls of the dead". "Clearly that shining insight is a revelation ... a logical consequence ... a perception swimming up from the unconscious". "Obviously our present existence is one of a long series of incarnations ... an illusion ... our sole chance at life". "Man is inherently good ... a sinner ... a mixture of both ... morally neutral". Such doctrines provide the skeleton for all our knowledge. They are not conclusions from observation and reasoning, but the very framework that sustains the movement of our thought. And every step we take toward the ultimate is influenced by that theological or proto-theological framework which develops and changes throughout our lives, although not, for the most part, suddenly and radically.

Our explicit or implicit theologies lead us to expect certain experiences and not others. And we make sense out of our experiences by referring them to that framework, fitting them into the pattern we already have. It is not unknown for a person to deny the reality of an event or a spontaneous response because he cannot find a place for it in his mental structure. "It's too horrible—it can't have happened.... It's too strange— it can't be true.... There is no such thing as telepathy—faërie—spirit—therefore the events which persuade the credulous to believe in them can be dismissed out of hand." Here, our rational categories are limiting what we are able to perceive. At the other extreme, we admit all appearances indiscriminately, eschewing intellectual standards and making no effort to correlate and evaluate our experiences. The framework for our experience becomes flabby and diffuse and our intellectual life degenerates toward chaos.

Neither of these extremes is tenable for those of us who accept ourselves as social, as well as individual, beings. But are we that? How do we know that the concept of "person" with which we began this study is correct? In an absolute sense, we do not know. It is useful as a starting-point; that is all. The proposal that our fulfilment lies in the scope and balance of all we are and do may be a false ideal. We must, however, start with a reasonably definite point of view—somewhere, not nowhere or everywhere. Practically speaking, this concept of "person" is as good a place as any to begin, and better than some because it requires us to remain flexible until we have some confidence that the way we are on is the right way for us. Later we may move to a new basis. For example, we may commit ourselves to one of the special ways of asceticism or ecstatic transport, or adopt the definition that individuality is an illusion. Even such mind-negating disciplines as some forms of Buddhism, however, require of their students a preparatory phase of intellectual training. Therefore a novitiate devoted to fostering and correlating a wide range of our capacities will leave us free to go on into either an ordinary or an extraordinary life, when—or if—we are called to decide.

Meanwhile, intellectual problems do arise, and we must settle them at least provisionally in order to continue our prayer and worship. From the earliest phases of our spiritual life, we alternately kneel and stand. We are transfixed with wonder; when the moment fades, we rise to our feet, telling ourselves, "This was from God", or asking ourselves, "Was this from God?"

Any beginning student of philosophy could inform us that this is the sort of question that comes late, rather than early, in logically organized discourse. All sorts of preliminaries should be considered first, like the nature of knowledge, the analysis of thought processes, the meaning of our words. The objection is valid but irrelevant. Here we are not building a philosophical system but engaged in practical living, and whatever *our* question happens to be is the correct one for *us* to work on, whether it is the metaphysical problem "What is ultimately real?" or the epistemological problem "How do we know?" or the historical problem "Who was Sākyamuni?" or the psychological problem "What is happening to me?" Any intellectual difficulty which rises out of our worship or blocks our worship will give us our proper point of departure.

Because the question emerges within a context, our answer must finally refer back to that context—a requirement that is all too often forgotten, and when forgotten, not infrequently results in "a position at once unanswerable and intolerable . . . complete in theory and crippling in practice".[1] To take a quite simple example: a mystic believes that he has directly encountered the ultimate, and discusses his vision with an analytic philosopher and a psychiatrist. The philosopher pushes him until he acknowledges that in describing the event, he is using words, concepts, and logical relationships which he cannot precisely define, and which exhibit internal contradictions. The conclusion seems inevitable that the mystic does not really know what he is talking about, so there is no point in further discussion of this nonsense. The two are left

170

with the mystic's vision on the one hand, and the philosopher's intellectual structure on the other, but no way to bring them together.

Similarly, the psychiatrist refers the mystic to various mechanisms of psychological needs, emotional stress, and environmental pressure, employing categories that refer always to the individual in his natural setting, but he does not come to grips with the mystic's overwhelming sense that in his experience, he has met something utterly beyond the mundane. Both analysts begin with the account of the experience, but neither returns to it. The one has cut off communication with the mystic by his linguistic critiques, and hence has no access to the event itself. The other denies, a priori, the reality of the event. Thus neither can share with the mystic his investigation into the authenticity, meaning, and significance of that mystical vision.

When a spiritual event is reduced to its psychological and philosophical components, the spirit escapes, for the same reason and in the same way that life escapes from a body when it is reduced to a little pile of inorganic elements. Physical chemistry can tell us only what the body is made from, not what the body—much less the embodied person—is. Psychological analysis can describe the equipment we have at our command and the limits within which we function—our personal characteristics—but it does not identify who we are. It may be able to explain how we perceive, but it must take our word for it when we tell what we see. The source of decision and the center of responsibility—the self—is like biological life in being irreducible to simpler elements. Vital, personal, and spiritual phenomena cannot be subsumed under organic and logical headings. Rather, we must start from the other direction, with the whole person, and never in our study of its parts lose sight of the whole.

We can analyze our spiritual experience out of existence by demanding that words be used only denotatively and never figuratively. We can isolate it by treating it as an untouchable mystery. But spirituality need not be treated in these ways. It can instead be fruitfully explored by recognizing that language is a mode of participating, and is all but infinitely flexible in its denotative, connotative, informative, evocative, interrogative, and other functions. The inquiry into how propositions are related to one another can be made secondary to an inquiry into how language supports, enhances, and clarifies experience or, on the contrary, can darken and destroy it. Which contexts call for direct discourse and which for talking figuratively? Which call for poetry, for prose, for mathematical symbols, for rites that do not answer questions but that satisfy a hunger? When can we legitimately resort to myths and parables, and when should we eschew them?

Even in our private thinking about ultimate matters, we shall find ourselves using a variety of languages for various purposes. Both for our increasing perceptiveness and for communications with other persons, sooner or later we shall need to learn to differentiate the various functions that language serves, and discover what each function will and will not do. Specifically, we must determine what functions the rational, objective intelligence should perform, and which are beyond its range.

One of its functions is immediately apparent: to discern how the many levels of our existence are related to one another, and if some are out of harmony with others, to find in what ways and to what extent we can integrate them. Our emotions and reason seem to be at odds? We know full well that we have no good reason to fear something-or-other, yet we are fearful of it? The intellect identifies the situation, notes the contradiction, considers what we can do about it. It may call for re-thinking our faith, for re-directing our behavior, for replenishing our store of images, or living quietly with the contradiction for the time being.

Some matters are amenable to philosophical treatment; some are not; and it is one of the major services of the intellect to determine when one of our other abilities should be called into play. To know when not to think philosophically, but instead to imagine, worship, observe, or play, and to know when not to resolve a tension or dissect prematurely a nascent idea, contribute as much to wisdom as the most penetrating logical and linguistic studies.

A fundamental limitation of the intellect in spiritual matters has been admirably stated by C. S. Lewis in his novel *Till We Have Faces*: "Holy places are dark places. It is life and strength, not knowledge and words, that we get in them. Holy wisdom is not clear and thin like water, but thick and dark like blood".[2] Our concepts and categories cannot be limited to the precise, clean world of ideas when we are wrestling with demonic powers rather than juggling with philosophical abstractions, or when we are fighting to order our whole existence instead of merely organizing our thoughts. On the other hand, intellectual disorder is of no help in living spiritually (or mundanely, either), or in discovering whatever order may be inherent in

173

life, or discriminating between the potentially fruitful and the barren.

What we know of the "dark places" comes to us in the form of images more often than in the form of ideas, and such control as we have within that realm is wielded by means of images. Much of the power of every religion springs from its ability to impregnate us with images, or to liberate them from deep within us, and to relate them one to another in a manner that unites all the aspects of ourselves with the ultimate.

We do not consciously and deliberately generate the potent images that in fact direct much of our lives. They arise out of the darkness. Our minds can fabricate illustrations and allegories, but images appear as if they were given to us—and in some cases undoubtedly they are. Stories, ceremonies, works of art, attitudes of respect and contempt among our associates, our daily interactions with the world—many things contribute to our vocabulary of images. We have little choice, if any, over which shall appeal strongly to us and have an integrating power over other images: Home or A Far Country, the Young Hero or the Mother Goddess, the Sacred Tree or the Holy Grail, Yahweh the Creator or Kali the Destroyer. We do have choice, however, of how we shall use those images and the forces they represent.

Images are controlled not by abstract ideas, but by other images. Thus metaphysical arguments about free will, and scientific arguments about the existence of "spirits", are useless in helping a person who believes himself to be possessed by a demon. But the intellect is not therefore helpless. It clarifies and enlarges the situation by recognizing that if evil spirits can exist, so also—presumably—can spirits of good.

174

Therefore, the way to approach the sufferer may well be by calling on angels and ministers of grace against the demon. *We* may not believe in demons or angels, but the sufferer does, and we must meet him where he is. A rite of exorcism may be employed to reinforce the imagery of human persons as responsible participants in a battle between good and evil powers in contrast to persons as lonely, impotent victims of extra-terrestrial fiends. The image of the devil is neither rejected nor allowed imperium. It is disciplined by countering it with an opposing image.

Which positive images will be effectual for us, we shall discern as we seek for them: against the fiend perhaps not an angel, but instead any of a thousand other images: the archetypal Wise Old Woman, the stars in their courses, a deity, a strain of music. The ongoing natural life around us can itself be a powerful image of and for life or death, stability or change.

The scrupulous intellect accepts as fact that to a considerable extent we live by images as much as by ideas, but it rightly demands that our images be consistent with each other and with our experience of life. If persons are wholly masters of their fate and captains of their souls, how shall we account for our seemingly uncontrollable urges and thoughts, our failures, our limitations? If human beings are inherently cooperative and loving, why do we find it so difficult to live together in harmony for more than a brief time, or except under highly controlled conditions of membership and physical circumstance? If we are not merely born to become saints, but born already sanctified, why have we fallen so low? If our basic nature is bestial, how have we risen so high? We explore the possibilities with every shred of our intellectual resources, searching theology, the sciences, literature and legend, and our own hearts, for clues to a synthesis.

Our immediate purpose is not logical consistency, but imaginative coherence. Later we may want to distill a theological system out of our working synthesis; as novices, what we need is a pattern that works both to satisfy us inwardly and to relate us satisfactorily with the world. Employed with discretion, logical criticism and system-building can provide invaluable clarification of what we are doing, revealing gaps that need to be bridged, problems that need to be investigated, contradictions that need to be resolved.

For myself, I know of few disciplines more productive for integrating spiritual and intellectual life than occasionally writing down my current creed or statement of faith. Where do I stand? What do I really believe at this point in my development? Where am I now? By laying out the design in words, I am prevented from resorting to my usual evasions and obscurities. Admittedly the words are inadequate, but then, a framework always is, and this technique is meant to expose the skeleton of the organization of my thought. This way I can make more sure that— so to speak—my sculpture of the human person does not have its eyes in the soles of its feet and a hand growing out of its skull—unless, of course, I intend to portray him so and intend to live as if humanity were made in that image.

Two results are likely to follow when we have correlated our ideas and images into a coherent picture, and tentatively defined their relationships. First, we realize that while we have not chosen the images that speak to our condition, assessment of their meaning is largely a matter of our making choices. Second, we confront squarely our responsibility for what we take to be real and true—what we live by. Do we attribute our moments of wonder (or anxiety or desire) to physical, psychological, or spiritual sources? We can describe them in these terms and many more. Consequently, we not only can, but must, decide how to take them, and live with our choices, and be prepared to replace them if we find them unlivable.

Those choices need not be capricious. We can and ought to examine the implications of each. If spiritual phenomena are purely natural, why do we persistently feel that they point beyond themselves? If they are intimations of the ultimate, how can the transcendent work through natural processes—and if it can, why does it? We trace implications and anticipate objections, but the further we go, the more obvious it becomes that the evidence and the arguments will not make up our minds for us. We carry to our graves the burden of decision, lightened only a little by the plea, "But I was never taught that there are other possibilities! It never occurred to me to raise that question!"

Nowhere do the great religions differ more conspicuously than on whether the worshipper is obligated, or even permitted, to think. Generally they appear to agree that when an intellectual question spontaneously arises, we can take some initiative in seeking out an answer. Some traditions concede that any question is permissible, but declare that questioning is at best irrelevant and should not be encouraged. Others contain within their web of belief the theme that thinking and questioning to the limit of one's ability is itself praiseworthy. Although historically that po-

177

sition has not always been dominant in the West, it has persisted at least since the time when the drama of Job was written.

Every person who enters the life of the spirit must decide, sooner or later (and probably sooner), whether his intellect is to be left outside or brought inside. By now my position should be sufficiently clear: the very writing of this book testifies to my conviction that intellectual activity is consonant with spiritual development, the only limitation being the general rule which applies to all mental life: intellectual operations must be appropriate to the material under examination. We do not use the same techniques for analyzing a chemical compound and a poem, or investigating a social structure and a new medium for painting.

Abstract ideas call for pure, detached rationality, living images for participatory, practical reason. For the life of the spirit, even such an exercise as creating a theological system will often—not always—have a pragmatic motive and achievement: the clearing away of confusions and contradictions that are thwarting our approach to the ultimate. And the decisive test of our intellectual efforts will be how well they succeed in correlating the entire range of our experience, reflection, and action with our life in the spirit.

The only counsel I can give to those whose obedience to the ultimate calls them to abandon the intellect is that they take a guide within that tradition. Little that I can say will be of any use to them. Theirs is a way that I can respect, but not one I have tried even briefly to follow, and I confess to some doubts concerning its value except for people who wish to use it as a temporary discipline, or those who are simply not interested in thinking or are unable to think. Conceivably their spirituality can be as intense and exalted as that of a saintly scholar; it is not, however, as comprehensive. Less of the person, less of the world, is brought explicitly under the aspect of eternity. At the same time, the risks to the person and the world may be less because everything which is open to the possibility of salvation (in whatever sense) is equally open to the possibility of damnation. Or the risks may be greater, as when the gullible follow a cultist to their doom, a case in point being the Jonestown mass suicides. The way of excluding the intellect is, I believe, easier if not necessarily safer than the way which includes our full mental powers. But we do not choose between the acceptance and rejection of the intellect on the basis of ease or safety. Here again we have the question of vocation: what are *we* called to do and become?

The call will vary not only from person to person, but also from time to time. The most simple-hearted will occasionally be afflicted by an intellectual perplexity; the most theologically-minded will have periods when he rests from his intellectual labors. A general trend, however, will become apparent as we proceed, if it is not already clear at the time when we are entering the life of the spirit. Our wonder spontaneously excites our curiosity, or it does not; our worship naturally serves as a refuge from excessively intellectual preoccupations, or as an opportunity for intellectual nourishment and stimulus. Apart from the special requirements of a particular religious tradition, there is no universal law to the effect that we must or we must not, at any stage, examine our beliefs, study the history of our tradition, deliberate on what we are doing when we pray, or construct a theology.

• • •

Study and meditation are the two basic activities by which we lift our minds to a competence commensurate with our worship. What we study need not be confined to "religious" or "spiritual" subjects: any subject will do if it trains us in scrupulous accuracy, and develops standards and habits which will color all our intellectual operations. To be rigorous in scientific argument but slovenly in discussing politics, exact in art but careless in history, displays a fundamental lack of discipline. The norms of precision and comprehensiveness differ in their application from one realm of discourse to another, but rarely are such applications so abstruse that we must be experts in a field before we can identify circumlocution, pomposity, evasion, inconsistency, or broken chains of thought. We may lack the courage to challenge openly an instance of bombastic argument or slippery reasoning. We may not instantly recognize that data are inconclusive and language is misleading. But we shall not be deceived seriously or for a long time.

There are obvious advantages in undertaking an intellectual exploration of the history and theory of spiritual life. If, for example, we have learned that "the Dark Night of the Senses" and "the Dark Night of the Soul" are normal phases of spirituality, the information may not alleviate our distress when we are in those states, but will save us from drawing certain false conclusions about them, and our passage through them will more likely be productive of good. If we know who some of our predecessors were, we shall be more apt to recognize companions among our contemporaries, and less prone to mistake mountebanks for wise and discerning teachers.

Spiritual functions, like physical, intellectual, emotional, and moral functions, are subject to evils of excess, defect, and perversion. Not everyone is called to prolonged or profound investigation of these evils, but we should know something about them in order to defend ourselves from the worst. For example, extensive learning about spiritual evil can be dangerous for anyone not well along in his spiritual development. With no learning about evil at all, however, we shall spend far too much energy repeating old mistakes, following leaders who have long been discredited, and laboriously pulling ourselves out of pitfalls that we could have avoided painlessly with an instructor.

Study is active and outgoing. Meditation is also outgoing, but its activity is of another kind. When we meditate upon an object, event, idea, person, we focus our attention upon it to search out its relationships with the ultimate, and establish it as a channel of communication with the ultimate. Typically, though not invariably, formal or informal study precedes meditation. We have learned what the prophet said, what situation he was speaking to, what the alternative translations are, and mastered the text as far as we are able. Or as Avery Brooke describes, we observe carefully a stone or picture or seed-pod.[3]

Now, meditating, we consider what it may be saying to us individually or to our time and society, about the final things. The coffee cup in our hand can tell us of the creative hands that shaped the clay, of the creative processes in the universe, of the ritual use of cups, of the refreshment conveyed by drinking, of the refreshing gifts we receive for body and spirit from the ultimate sources of life, and how they come to us. Emptying our minds and desires of all else, we consider the enigmatic line of poetry, the paradox, the solemn mystery, the person of the saint, a commonplace event or object, diligently exercising both our analytical and our imaginative abilities as a way of opening ourselves to the ultimate, of breaking down our resistance to wonder.

Obviously there are theologies, arts, liturgies, deeds which grow from roots other than wonder, and properly are measured by other criteria: pictures, poems, and stories designed to instruct, convert, or entertain, theologies to meet philosophical objections, religious rites to satisfy emotional or cultural needs, good works to comply with ethical demands. These can all be richly productive, but their product is not designed primarily to introduce the ultimate into nature and humanity, or to reveal it as already there. They are born of the mundane, not of the ultimate, so they do not concern us here except as we acknowledge their high calling, and often their high achievements. What springs from wonder, however, and is directed to enhancing wonder, is tested by its power to quicken us spiritually and to integrate all our functions with the ultimate.

In that process, we depend heavily upon the intellect to correlate the realms of the mundane and the transcendent in such a way that each fulfils itself in its relations with the other. How they are to be related, we decide for ourselves: whether we shall receive the mundane as real or illusory, and whether the goal of our lives shall be the separation of spirit from body or their coinherence.

Our worship is directed by our beliefs, and our beliefs are modified by the insights of meditation and the intuitions of wonder. It has been supposed that since the fruits of wonder—worship, praise, adoration—are central for all the major religions, therefore the differences among religions are trivial. So long as we worship sincerely, does it matter *what* we worship? If spiritual life were a quality of responsiveness, rather than the establishment of a relationship, sincerity would be enough. The nature of a relationship, however, is determined by the nature of the other as well as by our own nature. Therefore, ultimately not to know or not to care what we worship is a sign of wanton irresponsibility—a denial of our fateful involvement.

Our knowledge may be principally negative: for example, the ultimate whom or which *we* worship is not (or is) a machine, or a lover of cruelty, or capricious; nor is it this, that, or the other deity. We may (or may not) try to formulate our more positive insights and intuitions into what the ultimate is, in order to know the ultimate more intimately. But to know is not to possess, despite our tendency to assume that once our ideas are sufficiently complete and precise, we shall have captured the thing itself, as if to know a person's name were to know who and what he is, or as if clarity of mind were sufficient to purify the heart.

The awareness of the ultimate is intuitive rather than intellectual, but unless our intuitions are confirmed intellectually as well as in behavior, they will be in danger of degenerating into a malignant emotionalism. The main functions of intellect in the life of the spirit are to enhance wonder and to remove what inhibits wonder. We seek to understand in order to praise more accurately. The suggestive power of our knowledge, therefore, is at least as significant for worship as our acquisition of specific information.

What we learn gives us a vantage point from which

we can look, as from the crest of a hill, toward what we do not know, and the higher we climb the mountain of knowledge, the wider the vista—but also, the more we may be tempted to pride ourselves on our accomplishments rather than to marvel at the vision. All questions may be legitimate, but not all times are appropriate for asking and answering them. Worship which is devoted to explanations or limited to what is already intelligible, forfeits the blessing of a mind enriched by what is not yet comprehended. Refusing wonder, we grow intellectually arrogant and then sterile.

Returning to the question "What or whom do we worship?", we may be able to see now that the question cannot be answered by a clear, definitive, philosophical statement, because it does not represent a philosophical problem. We do not postulate a god to provide a terminus for an infinite regress of causes or of knowledge, or to explain why things happen as they do, or to give us hope for the future. We simply acknowledge the ultimate that we have met directly in wonder and worship, indirectly by other means. "Why do you need a god?" a theologian was asked once in the midst of an argument. He answered, "I don't, philosophically, any more than I need you for my philosophical structure. But having met you, I cannot deny your existence or how you affect me."

Although we do indeed learn about ourselves when we approach the ultimate, more significantly we learn who or what is meeting us. Not least is our discovery that we can grasp only a tiny fraction of what is there, and every time we come to rest on the certainty that finally we comprehend its essential being, it surprises us again by revealing a new aspect of its nature—and thereby a new understanding of ourselves. Its capacity for breaking our complacencies and startling us anew into wonder is as infinite as its power to produce, out of the ruins of our old lives, a new creation.

I myself refer to the ultimate as a person because its invasion evokes from me a personal response, penetrating farther into the core of my being than anything else does. Thus our relation is intrinsically, piercingly personal, its thrust generating a new kind of personal life. The impregnation changes my ideas because it changes me.

Others respond impersonally to the ultimate, whether because it approaches them from a different direction, or because of their own kind or degree of receptivity, or for some other reason. Between us there is disagreement, but need not be antagonism. How deeply we can communicate with each other, however, is open to question.

We do in fact become more and more like what we worship, and between personal and impersonal beings, interchange is necessarily limited. I can see how being a person, and the particular person I am, divides me from other persons and from things, and in rare flashes, I can see how blessed it would be to merge indistinguishably with them, in a life encompassing us all "as a drop of water in the ocean". Once I experienced utter annihilation of my self and its utter fulfilment simultaneously, and since then, I am not sure that they are incompatible.[4] Still, if my ultimate longing is not finally answered from an ultimate source, if the object of my worship is not fully responsive, if whatever enables me to become a person is not personal, then as I see it, there is a rift in the universe that strikes to its heart, a fundamental incoherence that I find intellectually as well as spiritually intolerable.

Because reason can clear the way for awareness and vision, although their source is not rationality, we have here the archetypal problem of how to correlate kneeling with standing, prayer with its critique. The ultimate has met us, and if it cannot be confined in such categories as "personal" and "impersonal", yet we must use the categories we have if our experience is to be integrated into our lives, instead of being isolated in its private cell.

What follows is the long work of testing each against the other: falling to our knees and rising to our feet, accepting the need for alternation as naturally as we do the fact that physically we cannot kneel and stand at the same time. While we are kneeling—literally or figuratively—we open or offer ourselves without trying to define what we are doing or why, or to define the ultimate. When we are again on our feet, nothing is exempt from our examination, and from our effort to relate the vision to all that we know, have, and are.

Standing, our minds function as judges but not as executioners, to evaluate but not to destroy the awareness. What we have felt and seen is authentically *our* response and perception, which we may properly test for what it is not, in order to discern what it is. To attack the sight or the thing seen, however, to require that it prove itself against scientific or logical criteria that were never meant for such a purpose, leaves us with only a corrupted memory. Rather, our intention is positive: to discern what is going on. When we have determined that our awareness is not a product of addled digestion or a relic of infantile fantasy, we shall still have before us a number of possibilities including, for example, that it was a purely psychological event arising from within us, or a spiritual event having its source beyond us. How can we choose between them? What methods will provide a sound basis for confirming one and rejecting the other? For that matter, why must we elect one to the exclusion of the other? Cannot we have both—or hold the matter in abeyance and be frankly agnostic?

We cannot have both because they are mutually exclusive. Agnosticism is theoretically admirable, but practically untenable because it is a position that we cannot *act* upon. Frequently it makes no difference in our behavior whether we have encountered the ultimate or merely have discovered some hitherto unknown facet of ourselves. Then suddenly we find ourselves in a situation where we will behave in one way if we take it that we are submitting to a psychological pressure, another if we take it that we are called by the ultimate. The one can be brushed off, or handled by psychological methods. The other cannot. The path forks, and we cannot take both or neither. Nor can we stand indefinitely trying to make up our minds. We must act—turn toward New York or San Francisco. At the next intersection, we may choose the other alternative: no one commitment is necessarily decisive for the rest of our lives. Yet there is no evading those decisions. We can be agnostic in our thinking but not in our actions. We do, or we do not, kneel.

Throughout our spiritual lives, we shall be tormented by what T. S. Eliot calls "The demon of doubt which is inseparable from the spirit of belief".[5] Our first defense against that demon is the knowledge that this happens to us all. Our second is the determination to take those doubts as revelations of where our intellectual structure or our personal commitment is inadequate, and therefore as occasions for tearing down in order to rebuild more strongly or beautifully. Make no mistake: both the dismantling and the reconstruction are likely to be painful. One of our props is knocked out from under us and we fall with a thud.

But how else can we diagnose what needs mending? And how can we mend it unless we know where and how extensive the weaknesses are? If we attempt to evade or mitigate our doubts, to brush them off as enemies of our faith, we shall be left with a structure that will collapse when the real storms come, and meanwhile we shall not have mastered the tools and the skills for building again. We acquire those skills by practice and experience; therefore when doubts arise, let us work our way through them.

We are asked, "How can you Christians believe such damned nonsense as the Virgin Birth?"—and we study the problem to find out how it does make sense, or until we are certain that it does not. If not, however, why have so many intelligent and learned people held that belief? Or the Zen master asks us, "What is the sound of one hand clapping?" In asking that, is he directing us to listen for the sound, or to use our minds in a way that is unfamiliar to us? In multitudinous ways, rationality itself is being attacked today: what use is it to argue with a terrorist, a paranoid schizophrenic, a person whose only aim in life is gaining and wielding power? We need not only to be aware that the reasoning mind has resources other than rationality—imagination, empathy, intuition, and more—but also to be adept in using them. We shall have no lack of problems—spiritual and mundane—on which to practice with our tools, and to acquire (or invent) new tools, until their use becomes second nature.

The invasion of doubt into our system of beliefs calls for us to re-examine them. More serious are the doubts that call for re-commitment. "I have done thus-and-so; therefore I am beyond the pale and God cannot love or save me". At that juncture, we have no alternative but to abandon our entire structure of belief, or to declare roundly, "Get thee behind me, Satan". With respect to the demons of doubt raised by the problems of evil and—worse—meaninglessness, we may not be able to do better than take to heart a comment that Charles Williams makes about John Wilmot, Earl of Rochester: "God, his passion cried, did not reveal his secrets to men; for God, his pride added, had not revealed them to the Earl of Rochester".[6] The only remedy for existential doubt is the existential affirmation "Here I stand".

"From foolish devotions may God deliver us!" wrote Teresa of Avila.[7] To some, all our wonder and worship will be foolish, because neither our methods nor our achievements are compatible with theirs. And why should they be? We are trying to answer a question they have not asked. We are living in a domain that is as different from theirs as art from accounting. Diverse domains can touch, or even overlap, but the techniques, criteria, and goals of one are not necessarily applicable to the others. Indeed, both art and accounting have room for wonder and can evoke wonder, but by very different means, and only when they conform to very different standards of excellence.

Those who simply do not comprehend what we are

talking about and trying to do are likely to have one particularly serious grievance against us: that we seem to have no standards of excellence or authenticity within our own domain. We do not exhibit our criteria for differentiating wise from foolish devotion, worship of the transcendent from the worship of idols or of mental constructs fabricated to our own liking, spiritual from mundane life, or authentic from spurious vision. Their criticism is not only valid, but important. In the sweet name of tolerance, we have repeatedly succumbed to the sin of intellectual sloth, and allowed all manner of corruptions to go unchallenged. Having no clearly articulated standards to measure ourselves against, we have not known—and have had no way of finding out—when we are asking the right questions and have understood the answers rightly. We experiment, but have no clear test by which to determine whether the trial succeeded or failed.

Transferring criteria bodily from one domain to another is a peculiarly vicious manifestation of intellectual sloth, as in, "We know that prayer is effective because in X number of situations where we prayed, the desired results followed, and in Y number where prayer was not offered, the results did not follow". Within a closed system, predictability is a valid criterion, but by definition, the life of the spirit is not a closed system, and the decisive element in it—the ultimate—is utterly beyond our calculations. The entire activity of prayer is vitiated by treating the absolute Other as a "known".

For evaluating forms of spirituality, the criteria of theological orthodoxy, sincerity, and exceptional experience are not much more satisfactory. Many other criteria have been proposed, but we do not have for the domain of spirituality anything comparable to musical or literary criticism, with their standards for evaluating performances and achievements. We can differentiate types, but not qualities, of worship, as the prayer of intercession from the prayer of thanksgiving, but not "foolish devotions" from those that are not foolish—as if, in music, we could not tell if the singer were off pitch or, indeed, were singing or merely making noises.

At the present, I can go no further than to suggest first, that if prayer evokes or increases wonder, or is compatible with wonder, we need not be troubled about it. It is not altogether a foolish devotion when it contains that element in any of its forms: amazement, awe, ecstasy, dread, or the sense of being in the presence of that which is infinitely, ultimately, transcendent. Wonder is not in itself spiritual, but always—I believe—when the spirit wakes at the approach of the ultimate, wonder enters. It must not be forgotten, however, that we can encounter the ultimate in ways other than worship and prayer, as in our dialogues with it, and our protests and self-assertions against it—again, remember Job. In such cases, wonder as such may be absent, yet we know that the one we are addressing is the same as the one before whom we kneel at other times—as we recognize our beloved as the same person when we are hotly arguing with him and when we are finding solace in his arms.

A second criterion for identifying devotions that are not foolish is that in practising them we are not attempting to use the ultimate as a tool. We may ask, beg, plead, praise, but we do not demand, nor do we instruct the ultimate what to do or how to do it. And I suggest also a third criterion: in prayer that is not foolish, we do not know or seek to know; we submit to being known. Beneath all the actions of praying, from simply directing of our attention to our physical behavior, lies the intention to submit, to be known and used.

It is very tentatively that I propose wonder, openness, and submission as possible criteria for authentic spiritual life. None of them is of much use in evaluating the worship of another person: how can we know what freight his words, gestures, and actions are carrying? But they may serve as guidelines for ourselves. It will be noted that none of these criteria is even remotely connected with intellectual ability or training. Although all our intellectual resources can be used in spiritual development, that way is as open to the unintellectual and the unintelligent as to the most brilliant scholar—and the simple may, in fact, outstrip the sophisticate spiritually. The latter may be so cumbered with the riches of the mind that, like Naaman when he was told merely to bathe in the Jordan to cure his leprosy,[8] he has trouble accepting such a simple requirement as wonder. Always the competent are tempted to take charge rather than be taken charge of, and to know without being known. They are prepared to be martyrs but not to be fools.

The fundamental problem in relating the life of the mind with life in the spirit is not how much intellect we possess, but how we use what we have. If much, we are not in a specially favorable position; if little, we are not under any disadvantage. "Our handicaps are all different, and the race is equal. The Pharisees can even catch up the woman with the mites".[9] The ultimate is equally available to us all, whatever our abilities and education, whatever work we are doing, and whatever our place in the world.

CHAPTER EIGHT

The Life of Action

It is something to be sure of the deed; our courteous Lord will deign to redeem the motive.

Charles Williams
The Figure of Beatrice

The life of the spirit is centrally and essentially a life of action. Spirituality is something *done*, not merely something believed or known or experienced. The spiritual is not what is left over after matter has been subtracted, but the glorification of the world infused with the holy, and the primary function of spiritual living is to facilitate the penetration of the holy into persons, processes, and states of affairs. All our praise and intercession, thought and argument, waiting and receiving, are only ways of carrying out that work. Prayer itself is work. But also, work is work—and here I mean by "work" whatever we do in relating ourselves with our natural and social worlds, whether it be paid or unpaid, and whether done from love or from necessity.

In this discussion of the life of action, moral precepts and questions of good and evil will be peripheral. Goodness and holiness are not the same, and for spiritual life, goodness is not enough because it does not lead directly to the ultimate. An atheist can be as good a person as a saintly believer in a deity: as perceptive morally, as swift and sure in acting upon those perceptions, as steadfast in adhering to his ethical norms. Atheist and saint may agree on what is right in particular instances or in principle, but they act from different understandings of the world, and seek different goals. While by definition the saint is good, a person can be supremely good yet not a be saint.

Briefly, the virtuous person has committed himself to righteousness; the holy one has given himself to the ultimate. The authority for the one is a principle such as the greatest good of the greatest number, or a rule or set of rules such as the Ten Commandments, or a norm such as love or loyalty. The reference for the other is the ultimate whom he knows in wonder and worship. No more than the artist can the saint work by formula, or express his principles in a code. Both artist and saint are governed, in the end, by their sense of the fitness of things, and although either may be able to give other reasons for what he has done, these are almost always *ex post facto* descriptions rather than prior grounds for acting in one way instead of any other.

An incredible quantity of bad art and bad living have resulted from following one's sense of the fitness of things, because that sense can be undeveloped, perverted, or enslaved by sentimentality, fanaticism, pride, or other of the sins. Fitness—appropriateness to the situation—depends upon the perception of some kind of order, but *what* order is perceived will depend upon a myriad of cultural and individual factors.

We are taught, formally and informally, what our tradition or particular teachers consider beautiful, intellectually sound, and socially appropriate. Our own experiences confirm or modify or supersede that teaching. If we have been well taught and have learned well, we shall understand that the rules of artistic color balance, of logic, of social organization, are not laws to be mechanically applied, but means for training our eyes to see clearly, our minds to think cogently, and our behavior to be felicitous. Likewise, the rules for spiritual living are not rigid precepts which, if meticulously obeyed, will produce a particular quality of life, but means for developing, clarifying, and strengthening our sense of how our lives cohere and coinhere with the ultimate, and for training us in what we need to do. But since the ultimate includes the mundane, how we live in the mundane not only reflects our relations with the ultimate but affects them.

Paralleling the distinction between holiness and goodness is the distinction between vocation and occupation. Our vocations constitute the work we are

195

called upon to do under the aspect of eternity, our occupations the specific tasks we undertake. These may have little or no connection, as in the case of a person who is called to compose music but earns his living as a night-watchman or a bookkeeper. Or they may be connected closely. A person called to the "cure of souls" may find employment as pastor of a congregation, a spiritual or psychological counsellor, a monk or nun, a writer, a teacher, a social worker, or any of a number of other activities through which he can directly practise his vocation.

But how do we discover what our vocation is? To a few persons, the call comes early and unmistakably. Some never discover it at all. Some mistake their occupations for vocations, or claim an ultimate authorization for doing whatever they happen to want to do. Many of us—most, I suspect—find ourselves, in the normal course of events, not just attracted but impelled toward a particular type of work, so that we engage in it willy-nilly whether circumstances are favorable or discouraging. The painter who is deprived of his paints still sees with a painter's eye. The "born" teacher or healer will practise these arts with or without professional training. Thus one of the marks—or tests, if you will—of whether we have found our vocation is our persistence in that activity over a considerable period. We are drawn to it, or if pulled away for a time, are irresistibly drawn back to it, or to some related activity, at every opportunity.

A second mark or test is that our involvement in such work breaks down barriers between us and the ultimate. We do not have to strain to see that what we are doing is done under the aspect of eternity; it is our natural way of relating ourselves not only with the mundane but also with the transcendent. From the Christian perspective, this is because—as Charles Williams puts it—"Dante was created in order to do his business, to fulfil his function. Almighty God did not first create Dante and then find something for him to do".[1] On this hypothesis, we do not have to *make* a place for ourselves in the world, but only to find the place that has been prepared for us—or for which we have been prepared.

This does not mean that once we have found our place, hindrances to our vocation will automatically dissipate around us. We may well be bombarded from without and within by forces that are attempting to thwart or deflect us, or to destroy what we are doing. The history of spirituality is pock-marked with failed vocations: here, someone who was discouraged by his intimates; there, someone else who submitted to emotional blackmail; everywhere, people with inadequate grounding in spirituality who did not recognize their calling for what it was, but treated it as a self-indulgence or an inconsequential aptitude to be set aside at the instance of any competing demand on their time and energy.

A third mark of a genuine vocation is its social consequences, although this can be difficult to interpret reliably. It is not uncommon for young artists and writers especially (but not exclusively) to be derided by their associates, but let an art critic or proprietor of a commercial gallery, or an editor or publisher, sponsor one or another, and the worker is justified among his fellows. The social innovator is likely to be treated with contempt until his pilot project demonstrates its value and practicality. What makes this test dubious is, of course, that recognition may not come until long after the person is dead—Van Gogh and Kierkegaard come immediately to mind. Thus if we fail to find anyone to urge us on, we need not summarily abandon our calling as inauthentic, but we had better examine closely whether this is indeed our vocation, and if the answer is Yes, whether we are going about it in the right way.

For a comparable criterion, we can look to the long-established religious orders, which ordinarily prescribe that the person applying for admission pass through stages of months, if not years, as a postulant and novice before taking even temporary vows, with another lengthy period before his final, solemn vows. All this while, both the applicant and the community he wishes to enter are testing his vocation, and either party may conclude that he has been mistaken in believing that the call was authentic. The social test can be as important as the individual test, although neither is infallible.

We should not be impatient to discern our vocations. Nor should we desist from engaging in occupations until our vocation is manifest. It may be necessary for us to undergo the discipline of steady employment in an occupation, and to learn a variety of social and technical skills, as preparation not just for carrying on our vocations, but even for realizing what it is. "In practice no one does his life's work unless he first becomes the man who is fit to do it. No one runs a race unless he first goes into the training that suits him, and cuts out of his life the things that impede him".[2] If it takes us half a lifetime—or more—to become fit for our vocation, so be it. Let us work at developing our natural capacities and our relations with the ultimate until our particular direction and mode of action become clear.

As a kind of footnote on how we do what we do in either vocation or occupation: a great deal of nonsense has been written on the theme "Whatever is worth doing at all is worth doing well". Much of it is to the effect that to do something well, it must be done meticulously—as if a letter to a close friend should be as carefully laid out as a manuscript for a publisher, or a family home with children kept as immaculate as the pictures in interior-decorating magazines. Many things are worth only a lick and a promise; which things they are, we must judge for ourselves, admitting that any of us may be idiosyncratic about something that we insist on doing faultlessly: the bed perfectly made, the flower-bed perfectly weeded, the desk perfectly organized, the dovetailing perfectly joined.

The idea that prayer is legitimate work has recently met with little favor, and the possibility or even desirability of either impregnating life with the ultimate, or revealing what is already there, has received little acceptance. Except when spiritual life proves itself in the immediate performance of beneficent actions, it is likely to be shrugged off as self-indulgent or illusory. As a bondslave to morality or social action, it has been tolerated as, at times, art has been decried but tolerated as long as it performed as the servant of a state or cause.

But the great human activities like morality and art and learning and spiritual life do not serve social ends alone. They have intrinsic value. As disciplines they are autonomous, although as personal functions they are deeply interrelated, each supplementing, correcting, and enriching the others. It is not by purely intellectual discriminations that we make moral or aesthetic judgements, yet such discriminations contribute to those judgements. Conversely, morality cannot take the place of intelligence, and neither can replace art.

Because the autonomy of spiritual life is so often challenged, we shall do well to probe more deeply into its relations with morality. Here again the analogy with art is illuminating. The function of the artist, according to Charles Morgan,

> is to enable vision in others. That is his supreme service to men. Not to persuade or compel or instruct them. Not to tell them what their vision should be. But by his vision, by his power to penetrate the appearance of things, to demonstrate to men that there is such a thing as vision; . . . the duty of an artist is not to impose his vision upon men but to open their eyes.[3]

What we do with our vision, how we use our newly opened eyes, takes us into the realm of social responsibility and therefore of morality, but these lie outside the artist's duty and power. If he attempts to go beyond his commission—if he defines and prescribes instead of pointing and describing—he becomes merely a propagandist. Similarly, the nature of spiritual life is to establish and maintain an interplay between the ultimate and all else. Incidentally it may generate new institutions, reform societies, and redeem individuals, but here again the action has passed out of the spiritual into the moral realm.

Ethically, such enterprises may be above reproach. Socially, they may be imperative. But they are not in themselves spiritual works, because they are not concerned directly, if at all, with our relation to the ultimate. The description of this difference does not imply an evaluation, a fact which would be more obvious if we were comparing plumbers with pianists rather than spirituality with morality. Nothing in the nature of things prevents a person from being a fine plumber as well as a fine pianist, but also, nothing requires it, and probably most people would agree that the world is a better place because both activities are carried on and, by and large, are performed by people having the requisite abilities and skills. Meanwhile, the person whose gifts and temperament direct him toward spiritual life is likely to be urged into plumbing, so to speak, while the work he is competent—and called—to do remains undone. A world without contemplatives would be as desolate as a world without artists or scholars—or plumbers, and morality itself is clarified and enlivened by the gifts of the spirit.

The active life of the spirit contrasts with other ways of life principally in two ways. The spiritual person does things that are different from what other people do, or he does the same things but they have a different significance. Thus C. S. Lewis, writing of the Arthurian legend, describes the Household of Taliessin by saying, "There is nothing to distinguish them from people outside the company except the fact that they do consciously and joyously, and therefore excellently, what everyone save parasites has to do in some fashion".[4] King Arthur rules; the servants prepare the food; Prince Gareth cleans the privies; Dindrane prays. But no act is done for its own sake. Each expresses the person's relation with the ultimate, and that in turn determines his relations with others both within the Household and outside it, and to the work itself. All know that they live from one another, and delight in that interdependence; therefore, every contribution they can make to the community becomes an offering of love.

Manual labor can signify degradation and be soulkilling. Or it can be soul-restoring, as for Emily Brontë, who "clung to her duties at the parsonage as visionary and contemplative men cling always to the discipline that they have cultivated as an enablement of their vision".[5] Intellectual labor, also, can be soulkilling or soul-restoring, and can be done under the aspect of eternity or as a purely mundane occupation. Or it can serve as a handmaiden to the lust for power, or as a pleasant if strenuous recreation, or as one among many tools in the service of our vocation.

The meaning of our activities is not inherent in them. Potentially, any action can carry any number of meanings not only to the person performing it but also to others who participate in or observe it. Thus what we intend as an act of praise or penitence or love can be interpreted by our associates as merely doing our duty, or conversely, what for us is ordinary behavior may appear startling to the people with whom we live.

Because actions carry so many diverse meanings, merely "to mean well", however sincerely, is not adequate for spiritually directing our interactions with other people, or with nature, institutions, the whole mundane world. Each of these has its special rela-

202

tionship with the ultimate, its own place in the ultimate order. In the rapturous glow of our vision, we may come to believe that we know what those places and relationships should be.

It can be laid down as a well-established principle, however, that seldom do we know what our peers ought to do, and our eager, well-meaning struggles to coerce them into the pattern we see for them will almost certainly be disastrous. "Everyone knows how terrible it is to come into contact with those people who have an undisciplined missionary urge, who, having received some grace, are continually trying to force the same grace on others, to compel them not only to be converted but to be converted in the same way with precisely the same results as themselves".[6] Or "under the guidance of the Spirit", we plan and execute social programs designed to provide for others what we are convinced is good for them, but may have nothing to do with their desires and needs.

A disciplined missionary urge is something else again. A person called to be a legislator or an educator, for example, takes on responsibility for deciding what laws shall be enacted or what material shall be taught. A parent must make many decisions on behalf of the children under his or her care. We not only do, but must, coerce our associates, if only by the fact that every action and inaction of ours limits some of their options, and enables others.

How we use our powers remains a problem throughout all stages of spiritual life, and that problem is not solved by deluding ourselves that we have no powers. They may not be exceptional; they may be wielded without our conscious knowledge or consent; but we have them. The short answer to the problem is that we use whatever powers we have under the direction of the ultimate. A longer answer begins with the reminder that what we do and how we do it are equally important.

What we shall do depends upon our personal characteristics, our circumstances, and our calling, and can include any activity from cultivating our own gardens, literally or figuratively, to setting forth to save the world politically, economically, and religiously. There are traditions that not only justify but prescribe the use of any means, even unto genocide, to achieve their version of "saving the world"; hence the various attempts to exterminate Jews, Armenians, Baha'is, and uncounted other religious and political bodies, as if their members had no status *sub specie aeternitatis* and were ineligible to attain such status. I am so far out of sympathy with this understanding of the relation of humankind to the ultimate that here I will do no more than mention it.

Yet this example brings into the open, unequivocally, the fact that it is in the realm of action, not of belief or knowledge, where our differences decisively separate us. It is not the believer's conviction that Jews or Christians, Moslems or Baha'is, Blacks or women, are ultimately (that is, under the aspect of eternity) inferior or accursed beings, that calls for counteraction from those who hold other beliefs. It is his behavior; his treating them as inferior or accursed. His thoughts are his own; his behavior is everybody's business because it affects the entire community not only in its mundane life but also in its communal life under the aspect of eternity.

Whether our counteraction against what we take to be intolerable is by intercessory prayer or by militant measures, or both, the one thing we must not do is to justify our action as "protecting God" or "avenging an insult to the Almighty", or any of their equivalents—an attitude well expressed by one of Charles Williams' characters, who says, "God has only us to defend his glory, and what will happen to that if we leave off killing?"[7] The ultimate, like the sky, is beyond protection and insult. All we can do is defend our way of life against other ways of life that jeopardize what we ultimately value.

Certain traditions prescribe specific means for opposing what they define as evil, from "Death to heretics and unbelievers" to unconditional passive resistance. More often, they permit a range of possible means within those extremes: "You may take arms against an enemy soldier but not against a civilian". Or "You may attack a political leader by voting or demonstrating but not by assassinating him". Or as an old woman is reported to have said on her sixtieth wedding anniversary, when she was asked if she had ever considered divorcing her husband, "Murder, frequently, but divorce, never!"

Thus we can have no general answers to how we should use our powers and for what, unless we are already committed to a tradition, and in the major traditions, the leeway for personal decision and action is enormous. It would be pleasant to have a less heavy responsibility, but no one whom I know of has ever claimed that one of the fruits of spirituality is pleasure. Joy, yes, but not pleasure.

I do not know of any tradition—Eastern, Western, or other—that encourages the contemplative who is living in the world to forsake his mundane responsibilities. Parents are cautioned not to neglect their children in order to live contemplatively, or breadwinners their task of earning bread, or citizens their civic duties. If they decide to leave the world, they must wind up their affairs as if in preparation for death, but the winding up must be done. How they fulfil their mundane responsibilities is a separate issue; the point is that somehow they must be fulfiled, not because the mundane is of more value than the spiritual, but because willy-nilly we are rooted in the mundane world. We are both creatures with bodies and members of communities, and we cannot build a lofty spirituality upon mundane irresponsibility.

As a way to begin living spiritually within the "marketplace": we can meditate, pray, reflect, either between or within our mundane activities. We can rise early, or otherwise arrange for an uninterrupted period during the day for our communion with the ultimate. We can say grace before or after meals, or preface our work with Sir Jacob Astley's prayer before the battle of Edgehill: "Oh Lord, Thou knowest how busy I must be this day: if I forget thee, do not thou forget me".[8] In his book *Prayers*, Michel Quoist gives an example of a meditation while riding on the subway[9]—not, one would think, the most favorable setting for prayer, but available for the purpose if we have the imagination and discipline to use it in that way.

We can facilitate such between-times prayers by summoning what the author of *The Cloud of Unknowing* calls "the cloud of forgetting":[10] For the moment, we cover up our immediate mundane concerns as a mountain peak is temporarily covered by a cloud, so that we are not distracted from our worship. It is a practice that in fact we engage in all the time. We lay down the book we are reading in order to answer the telephone, and when the conversation is ended, we return to where we left off. Or in the midst of a committee meeting, we glance at our watch, not losing the thread of the discussion but placing it in its temporal relations with what is going on elsewhere. In such ways, we can lay down the "book" of our mundane business, or glance toward the "watch" of the transcendent in order to recollect our relation to the ultimate.

More specifically, we can prepare reminders until praying between-times becomes habitual. The flower on the desk ... the burning candle ... the scapular worn under the clothing ... the talisman in the pocket ... whatever is convenient and, preferably, inconspicuous: parading our private observances tends to cheapen them. In contrast, other observances are meant as public affirmations, for example, the Moslem prostrations toward Mecca five times a day, and the sign of the cross drawn on the forehead of some Christians on Ash Wednesday. Another way of training ourselves is by selecting some ordinary sight or sound to serve as a reminder: a factory whistle, a glance out the window, the ring of the doorbell which may herald not just a visit but a visitation.

Praying, reflecting, meditating within our mundane activities—while we are doing them—has similar everyday parallels. Think of the ardor that informs every step of choosing and wrapping a gift for someone we especially love, or of the happiness that permeates all our thoughts and activities after we have received unexpected good news. Then think also of those times of grief when our every move is weighted down with our loss. Likewise, we can become conscious of the fact that everything that is exists under the aspect of eternity, that everything we do is done under the aspect of eternity. A good deal of the time, probably we shall pay no more—and no less—attention to that fact than we do to the fact that the sky is overhead, but because of it, we see things differently from the way we would if we had lived our whole lives underground, and differently from the way others, who have not shared that vision, see things.

Praying within our work cannot be approached as directly as praying between-times, because the activity of prayer is the reflection of an attitude, and attitudes are changed only indirectly. We can dutifully admire, for example, but we cannot compel ourselves to wonder. We can discipline ourselves to be polite but not to be compassionate. Wonder, compassion, and other such graces come out of a way of looking at the world—how we structure what we see and do. The craftsman who lives under the aspect of eternity hones his skills "to the glory of God" ... the pure in heart sees everyone, friend or stranger, as of eternal worth ... the youngster has a natural reverence for all living things ... and all these persons are doing what follows naturally from their world view. What they are doing is natural for them, but not necessarily automatic. I can well believe that the pure in heart go through a long apprenticeship during which they often forget that the people they are dealing with are eternally significant, and even when their world view is well established, at times they will have difficulty in according that status to some particular person.

We do not develop such habits and attitudes overnight, but over years, and we may never reach the exalted states that are described in much of the literature. If we are typical, our course will be wobbly, not just initially but for a long time. We start enthusiastically, then ease off. We resume our efforts, probably with a touch of guilt, then relapse again. With each repetition, our guilt grows until finally we give up with "I just can't do it" or "This is not for me". We shall do better if, after a lapse, we pick ourselves up like a courageous child learning to walk who takes the tumbles in his stride. In our spiritual novitiate, we are indeed children learning to walk, so of course we fall down frequently. Of course we cannot perform the feats that spiritual athletes and ballet dancers execute seemingly with ease—although they also fall sometimes, and do not feel disgraced. These may be occasions for seeing ourselves as clowns, flopping gaily around on our way from one side of the circus ring to the other, arriving there awkwardly, but what does that matter since we do, in time, arrive?

Only experience and experimentation will reveal which of the ways of behaving differently from others or from our previous behaviors are indispensable to us, and how we can correlate our differences with the activities of those around us. Explanations may smooth our way with others, or may not. We cannot always get our point across, or the attempt itself may require our displaying more of our inner lives than we are ready to reveal. Maneuvering our schedules—or theirs—may be easily effected, or it may prove impractical. We may be able to achieve the solitude we need only by gracefully declining others' offers to help us with routine chores. We may have to learn to meditate in snatches—a difficult art but by no means impossible. And in the end, we may find that our particular vocation does not require us to do anything at all which is overtly different from what our associates do. Instead, what we do has a different significance—which can make all the difference in the world, but not a difference that is obvious to the casual observer.

Whether we do different things or just do things differently, however, sooner or later it will become apparent that *we* are different—it is the contrast between doing and being. Our values are not the same as those of our associates. We know things that they do not know, and do not know what seems obvious to them. Our attitudes and interests betray us. In John Fortunato's image, we are exiles from the community at large.[11] Even if we are gathered with like-minded others, those are communities of exiles, and as such are liable to persecution. It may be as mild as "Don't be silly" or "He's a grand guy but he has some pretty odd ideas", or as stringent as incarceration on the ground of insanity. (Nowadays, fortunately, we are not likely to be burned at the stake or crucified.) Speaking practically, people whose dress or manners or accent or color or affiliations set them apart from the mainstream tend to be exiled, and the spiritually committed are not expected.

Since what we are suffuses what we do, we should not be unduly surprised by the jokes or taunts or rejections, any more than by the affirmations, the gratitude, the welcome from other exiles. I do not know of any effective way to meet these reactions except by counting the hurt and the healing both as part of the game. By saying this, I do not intend to minimize the hurt. Making new friends does not cancel out the pain of breaking old relationships, even—or especially—when it is the old friends who reject us, not we who move away from them. The loss is real, and in the case of intimate relationships, can be devastating, as when parents and children or husbands and wives are constrained to go their different ways lest they cease to be be able to live *sub specie aeternitatis*.

Such radical dissociations ought not to be undertaken without long and careful consideration. I know of nothing in the history of spirituality to justify an abrupt plunge from one way of life into a wholly different way, as is required by certain of the more extreme religious coteries which mistake an emotional glut for authentic spiritual growth. Sudden conversions do occur, but their consequences must be worked out by transforming, not repudiating, the selves we already are.

Such injunctions as "sell all that you have and follow me" do not require acting impetuously, or flagrantly disregarding other people. If, for example, after deliberation we find it necessary to part company with our family, let us do it as considerately as we can, and go no farther from them than we must. In any case, here as elsewhere the novice has no business indulging in extreme behaviors such as abandoning those who are personally or financially dependent upon him. Such actions may become imperative when he is spiritually mature, but even then they are not to be undertaken irresponsibly without due preparation.

The books on spirituality and the spiritual guides tell us mostly of the heights and depths, but little of the daily-ness of life under the aspect of eternity. They warn us against succumbing to pride, envy, avarice, sloth, anger, gluttony, and lust, but rarely against the error of evaluating our spiritual state or status by the frequency and intensity of our "religious experiences". Yet ultimately it is not our feelings or even our visions that matter. It is instead the quality of our actions. Again the parallel with love is instructive. If a man believes sincerely that he is passionately in love but treats his beloved abusively, we have good reason to question whether he really loves her. On the other hand, we describe persons as "loving" if characteristically they are sensitive to others' needs, and patient and compassionate, regardless of their emotional involvement and their current emotional states.

A notable mark of the spiritual person is that he translates his awareness of the ultimate into practical, everyday action, not only when he is all aglow but also when he is inwardly dull or darkened. He does not depend upon his raptures to keep him going. They are "the cherry on top", not the substance of his way of life. For spiritual living, it is not necessary to *feel* anything. But it *is* necessary to *know* something—the ultimacy of the ultimate—just as we know, without any particular emotional concomitants, that day and night succeed each other, that there are people living on the other side of the world, that we are persons. And it is supremely necessary to *do* something.

During our dull periods, we may feel as if we are only "going through the motions", but going through the motions has its place in spirituality as much as in love. To act lovingly is more important than merely to feel affectionate. To treat particular persons and things as having an ultimate place and significance is more important than to be rapt in contemplation of a diffuse holiness investing a generalized world. "By

212

their fruits ye shall know them".[12] However, unless the tree has strong, well-nourished roots, it cannot bear good fruit.

We have here a cycle in which prayer enables us to act *sub specie aeternitatis*, and the action drives us back into prayer, and thence into further action which is corrected and empowered by our spiritual retreats. At some stages of those retreats, probably we shall re-examine our knowledge of the ultimate and the world, exercising our theological as well as our practical intelligence, until the whole, being informed with transcendence, issues in the contemplative life. And by then we shall have fulfilled our novitiate.

CHAPTER NINE

The Life of Contemplation

He said not: "Thou shalt not be tempested, thou shalt not be travailed, thou shalt not be dis-eased"; but he said: "Thou shalt not be overcome."

Julian of Norwich
Revelations of Divine Love

Contemplative living is open to anyone who makes himself available to what is ultimate, and who works at establishing and developing his interaction with the ultimate. And it requires work: hard, disciplined, sometimes agonizing work. The end, no one can foresee. The most that can be said of the contemplative life is that it offers an incomparable richness in heights of joy and breadth of wisdom, as well as depths of suffering, but it does not promise mere pleasure or ease.

How to live contemplatively can be learned, but there is no set of techniques and no body of information that can be directly transmitted from teacher to pupil, and whose mastery will guarantee the result. In this it is comparable to learning to write. A teacher can inculcate knowledge of basic grammar, vocabulary, spelling, and punctuation, and perhaps how to write a best-seller, but not how to create a masterpiece that will endure for centuries.

Thus as contemplatives—apprentice or master— one of our essential disciplines is to discover or invent practices by which we can develop our own spirituality. For this, we shall need all the resources we can muster. The history of contemplatives will help us, although not, perhaps, as much as we expect, because so great a proportion of that history was written by and for monastics or hermits who were already well beyond their novitiate, and living in a situation especially structured to facilitate living that way. We who are not only novices but "living in the marketplace" may be able to adapt some of the monastic patterns to our ways of living, or adapt our ways to their patterns, with the obvious qualification that no doubt we shall have to substitute a wrist-watch alarm for the Angelus bell or the muezzin's chant, and make other, less obvious amendments.

Our surroundings, however, are so different from the monastic that we should not be surprised to find ourselves having to invent new patterns. "Inventing new patterns" may sound formidable, but in fact it is something that we do frequently and unthinkingly. Every time we respond to a situation with something

215

other than a stereotype, or modify a routine, we are inventing a new behavior.

Such inventiveness is all the more imperative because we cannot begin from where our predecessors left off in the life of the spirit. In many disciplines—science, philosophy, history, and more—we can continue what others began, and in our intellectual understanding of spirituality we not only can but should build upon what our forebears built. Living spiritually, however, starts from scratch in every single case—think of the analogy with learning to walk and talk. And as our mastery of those bodily and verbal skills means using our unique combination of anatomical and other endowments, so our spiritual development rests upon our use of our particular, individual capabilities. Since we cannot follow exactly in another's footsteps, we cannot help inventing new behaviors, so we may as well take advantage of that fact and enjoy it. Moreover, in a world where every blade of grass and grain of sand is subtly different from every other, we should expect that persons, being far more complex, should differ comprehensively.

In some ways, the contemplative in the world can learn more from the hermits than from the monastics. Members of a religious community are surrounded by others of like mind and direction. Their daily round is specified by the traditions of their order. The division of labor among them reduces the time each must spend in housekeeping, gardening, laundering, and earning their living.

In contrast, ordinarily the hermit lives outside any face-to-face community. He is friendly and caring with those whom he meets unavoidably, but rarely is he intimate with anyone except his spiritual director, and often his contact with that person is chiefly by letter. He may live in a one-room hermitage, but it must be kept clean and orderly, and in cold weather, tolerably heated. He must do his own housework and gardening, and unless he has an income from an institution or from individual well-wishers, he must earn enough to pay for what he cannot produce by himself, perhaps as a day-laborer or craftsman. On many days, his routine will be radically changed because of the weather, or the coming of invited or uninvited guests, or illness. His discipline of prayer, study, and work is not prescribed for him; he must work it out for himself—and there is amazing variety in the solutions that different hermits have developed.[1]

So it is with the contemplative in the world. He is surrounded mainly by people with other concerns. He has to attend to a myriad of mundane activities and relationships. And he must evolve a pattern in which those responsibilities are not neglected, yet which reserves adequate time and energy for his spiritual life. Appearances to the contrary, the monastics—even those in the active orders—may have less for our illumination than the hermits do.

Another obvious resource is a spiritual director or counsellor or soul friend. What Raïssa Maritain writes of the convert is equally applicable to the novice:

> [He] learns only little by little to know his real powers. He may begin by framing purposes out of all proportion to his real capacity. A holy and learned guide is necessary to him (and more learned than holy, says Teresa of Avila). This guide, if one is so

fortunate as to find him, will judge of the solidity and resistance of one's soul; will prevent activity inspired more by presumption than heroism, and will moderate it to avoid the collapse of a physical and moral energy insufficient to nourish great but premature desires.[2]

A spiritual director, however, must be chosen with great care, and not given ultimate authority in all matters. Judging from my own observation and from fairly extensive reading, most of the spiritual direction readily available at this time is of one of two kinds, or a combination of them.

The first reduces spirituality to psychology or philosophy. As a priest once told me, "A man goes to his minister with a spiritual problem such as how to pray. The minister listens carefully, and when the difficulty is explained, he asks the man, 'How are you getting along with your wife?'" Or the director works within a psychological or theological framework which consciously or unconsciously he imposes upon the inquirer. As Raïssa Maritain says,

It thus happens, because of psychological entanglements which are very difficult to avoid, that entirely human opinions come to hold in the mind of him who should practice "the art of arts" almost the same rank as those certainties touching upon supernatural life, and are set forth nearly on the same ground as those things which are required for the soul's perfection.[3]

218

The other kind of direction presupposes that the inquirer is already committed to a particular tradition, or else the director knows only his own spiritual tradition and so inevitably steers the inquirer along that track. Such directors can be invaluable once the person has committed himself to a specific way, for example, Buddhism or Christianity or Judaism or Hinduism, but they can harm the novice by prematurely narrowing the compass of his exploration. There is a Buddhist proverb that says, "If you meet a Buddha in the path, kill him". In contrast, one of Phyllis Bottome's characters speaks of

> what might roughly be called "love"; not
> of course a sentimental love: a far more
> impersonal and less individual emotion. I
> sometimes think that migratory birds may
> have it for each other. They fly in the same
> direction, and have never been seen to
> interfere with each other's flights.[4]

What, then, do we do if humanly we are on our own? Exactly what our forebears did when they were pioneering: the Hebrew prophets, the Desert Fathers, the first Franciscans and Discalced Carmelites, the first Protestants, Jane Addams and Dorothy Day. They used what was available, and what they could not use, they discarded. They were resourceful in adapting to new conditions, and tenacious in pursuing their goal. They fell flat on their faces in the mud and some died there, but others hauled themselves up, washed themselves off, and went on. They strayed from the road, chased will-o'-the-wisps, doggedly cracked their heads against stone walls. They founded new communities and created new institutions, of which a few succeeded and many failed. And it was they—including the failures—who mapped the country and carved out the roads for their successors.

But the achievements of the pioneers will be of little account if they are not followed by settlers, and we should note that the special talents needed for either vocation are likely to be unnecessary or disruptive for the other. We can experiment with both these ways of life during our novitiate, and we should. What balance is right for us? Maintaining and building up the homestead? Making frequent excursions away from a home base that other people maintain? Setting off alone or with a small party into a wilderness? I cannot stress too emphatically how important it is to be rooted, for achieving and maintaining a healthy spirituality. The truly great spirituals, like those I have named above, have always—as far as I can discover—worked within their native tradition or an adopted one, and however far they travelled from it, they cherished their roots.

Undoubtedly there exist spiritual guides who are alive to individual differences and, while themselves committed, are not bent on making converts. Ideally, such directors are also deeply familiar with other religions and with other patterns within their own religion, and so can open to the inquirer a wide range of possibilities. A novice who finds one of these directors is blessed indeed, but apparently they are exceedingly rare.

As novices, what can we expect during our novitiate? First, that at the outset we shall often be very much alone. Possibly, even probably, this will be a period during which we have only books to companion us.

Later we may find soul friends or a spiritual guide, but at the beginning most of us grope blindly, making our own paths to the ultimate. "Alone" does not necessarily mean lonely, however. What it does mean is doing something by ourselves, at our own speed and in our own manner, without interference from others. G. K. Chesterton contrasts "things we do not wish a man to do at all unless he does them well", like brain surgery or running a restaurant, with "things we want a man to do for himself, even if he does them badly", like "writing one's own love-letters or blowing one's own nose".[5] But there are things that we *must* do for ourselves, well or badly, if they are to be done at all, and one of them is embarking upon the life of the spirit.

How and when we started, we may never be able to specify. When we look back from a distant vantage point, we may be able to pinpoint an event or time as having been decisive—and then we may be mistaken. This is not because there is something inherently mysterious about spiritual awakening, any more than there is inherent mystery about learning to talk. In both cases, until we have made considerable progress, we do not have the conceptual and linguistic resources to understand the process or even to become aware of it as a process. Or even if we have the resources, we may not see the significance of what is going on until after it occurs, perhaps long after.

Second, we can expect that our course will not be steady. Times of richness will alternate with times of dryness, times of fervor with times of laxity. That is as it should be. As Charles Morgan writes,

> O proud, impatient Man, allow to Earth
> Her seasons. Growth and change require their
> winter

As a tired child its sleep. Thou art that child;
Lie down. This is the night. Day follows
   soon.
Wake then refreshed, wiser for having slept.
This is old nurses' counsel, and the gods',
For, if thou rest not, busy maggots eat
Thy brain, and all is dedicate to chaos.[6]

We need to be patient with ourselves—others—the world—the ultimate. Patient, but neither complacent when we are in the light nor desperate when darkness engulfs us. Patient with our impatience and restlessness: these are natural, and all but inevitable, responses to certain situations, and to chide ourselves for them—when they are appropriate—is not only useless but silly. Such misapplied self-discipline is a prime example of the effort to force ourselves into the mold of untroubled serenity that many people suppose to be *the* pattern of spirituality.

A few contemplatives are of that quiet kind. Most are not, or they come to it in old age at the end of a troubled life. Or it comes upon them occasionally like the calm in the eye of a hurricane. The person of a naturally tranquil disposition will naturally display that style of spirituality, but in Judaism and Christianity, at least, spiritual styles are as diverse as personality types, with turmoil far more common than placidity. We need only to look at Moses, Elijah, and Jeremiah; Maimonides and Paul of Tarsus; Augustine of Hippo and Francis of Assisi. For most of them—and most of us—a better model than the serene would be Jacob wrestling with the angel, and emerging from that battle changed in the deepest recesses of his being.

It may seem strange to introduce Jacob under the heading of patience, but the connection is not arbitrary. Jacob had the patience to fight through to the end. He did not give up when the going got rough, and he lived with the wound to the end of his days— the wound that each of us suffers in encountering the ultimate at the level which is ultimate for us. We must be patient enough not to give up a struggle too soon, but to fight it through in whatever form it takes: John of the Cross against the Dark Night and other hindrances, Francis of Assisi against some of his followers, Teresa of Avila and Thomas Aquinas against their ecclesiastical superiors, any of us against any of the principalities and powers, angelic or demonic.

Often, however, the decisive battles are not the fiercely dramatic ones where usually the issues are clear, but those consisting of what Rumer Godden calls "martyrdom by pinpricks",[7] such as the incessant confusions, unclarities, and uncertainties of every day, and the petty annoyances and frustrations that seem too trivial to lift into the ultimate. Perhaps they are, but we can make or break our life in the spirit not only in the major struggles but also on the level of daily-ness: the daily-ness of bringing up children (the feeding at two in the morning, the diapers, the inconsolable crying), of the office memos, the assembly-line, the insistent telephone, the sales pitch. What these call for is "earthy mysticism", in William McNamara's phrase,[8] in contrast to "rising above them" in some sort of pseudospiritual aloofness. The detachment which is a goal of mature spirituality means abandoning our self-interest in things and other persons, not denying them our respect and even reverence. We cherish them for what they are in themselves, without regard for what they can contribute to or take away from us.

Third, we can expect to change in unpredictable

ways. One of our interests will unexpectedly intensify, another diminish. This acquaintance will become an intimate and that friend will drop away. The serious may become playful and the playful, serious—or not. In all probability, we shall simplify our lives, but what form that simplification will take is impossible to foresee. It may mean hiring a house-cleaning service, or merely discarding knicknacks that no longer have even sentimental value but always need dusting. Or we may spend more time playing music and less watching television and movies. We may become more or less active in civic or political or church or synagogue or temple affairs. And for a while, we may intermit any of the activities we were previously involved in, only to return to them later.

During our novitiate, we need to remain—or become—flexible, like a young athlete who successively plays basketball and soccer, and skis and fences, doing each to the limit of his ability but not restricting himself—yet—to any of them. Now he is testing himself for what he is capable of, and for what most intrigues him. Similarly, the spiritual novice will plunge into solitary meditation and social action, study and prayer groups, music and silence, long prayers and short, regular schedules and extemporaneous exploits, from time to time until he finds what he is called to concentrate upon. The plunging is not in itself a sign of unsoundness, unless it is too violent, or too prolonged as may be the case when a person dashes from one religion to another in an effort to evade a real confrontation. Like the athlete, the spiritual novice cannot tell which technique is best for him unless he tries each whole-heartedly.

How long will it take for the serious athlete or novice to discover his métier, or choose which he shall devote his major energies to? All I can say with any assurance is that in most cases, the time before making a commitment that he intends to be permanent should be measured not in days or months, but in years from when he began in earnest to live contemplatively. He needs time for some of the personal changes to occur, as well as time to experiment and explore.

We should remember that during this time, the ultimate is not passive, or active but ineffectual. We question and are answered, although we may have to listen carefully to hear the answer and think long before we understand it. We seek and are found. We are nudged and prodded and shoved toward what will be *our* way when we are not being held back or redirected or squelched. "Amiable agnostics will talk cheerfully about 'Man's search for God'", writes C. S. Lewis and adds, "To me, as I then was, they might as well have talked about the mouse's search for the cat".[9] Francis Thompson witnesses to the same phenomenon in "The Hound of Heaven", and Charlotte Mew in "Madeleine in Church". But it takes time to learn to discriminate between the promptings of the ultimate and our psychological urgencies, between the demands of morality and the summons to holiness.

Fourth, we can expect opposition from those who do not comprehend what we are doing, as well as from those who do understand and are threatened by it. We unsettle them, which provokes some of them into hostility—not all, but some. I remember a choir director pleading with a choir that had lumbered through the rehearsal of an anthem: "Look, this is a hymn of *praise*. Lift up your voices—and your hearts!"—and how angrily stunned they were at finding him concerned with anything besides the notes. Somebody has defined the Christian's duty as "to comfort the afflicted and afflict the comfortable", but the comfortable detest being afflicted (who can blame them?), and they are likely to take as an affliction whatever threatens the even tenor of their ways, as they are in being confronted with a way of life that challenges theirs.

And we cannot avoid challenging them. With due courtesy, we may refrain from speaking about these most intimate concerns, but we cannot hide forever from our families, for example, our early rising, or from our friends that we have obscurely—if not conspicuously—changed. By being who we are, more than by doing what we do, we disquiet them, and the best we can hope for is that once in a while, one of the comfortable whom we have wittingly or unwittingly afflicted may of his own accord decide that here is something worth looking into.

If it is we who are being challenged, our problems will be of another kind. Are we attracted to the holy in all its manifestations or only to particular people who exhibit holiness? The two are not incompatible: most often it is through other people that we become aware of the ultimate in the first place, by way of either books or face-to-face meetings. But as C. S. Lewis makes clear in *Surprised by Joy*, we can be attracted to the persons while being repelled by what makes them what they are. "George MacDonald had done more to me than any other writer; of course it was a pity he had that bee in his bonnet about Christianity. ... Chesterton had more sense than all the other moderns put together; bating, of course, his Christianity".[10] Through them and personal friends who were Christian, finally Lewis found what they had found, joined that flock of migratory birds flying in the same direction. There was nothing inevitable, however, about his move, and many people never make it, whether to Christianity or any other tradition. They stop at the signpost and never go on to what it is pointing toward.

Opposition can also come from within ourselves. *Surprised by Joy* provides a graphic and not atypical illustration, the *Confessions* of St Augustine of Hippo another, Raïssa Maritain's *We Have Been Friends Together* a third, and in fiction—among many others— John Buchan's *Mountain Meadow*, Lewis *Perelandra*, Isaac Asimov's short novel *Profession*, and several of the novels of Graham Greene. Each of these details a person's struggle against his inner resistance to the claim of the ultimate upon him, an inner resistance that may be echoed by outer ones—family or friends, or the mundane "spirit of the time"—reinforcing the reluctance to change. Although none of us will be troubled in exactly the same way as the persons in these examples we can be heartened by knowing and knowing of others whose battles have been as long and arduous as so many of ours.

There have been and are those who have responded gently and sweetly to the ultimate, without internal or external resistance, but they seem to have left fewer records than those who had to struggle either before or after their commitment. Thus from the reports we have, it appears as if typically, we can expect a battle at some stage or, along the way, a series of battles on different issues, at different levels of our being, and with our assailants attacking us from different directions.

The last of the sources of opposition which I shall discuss here is the most difficult to describe. It comes from the opposite to what I have been calling "the ultimate", and may be conceived of as an alternative ultimate. We have, on the one hand, what we can only call truth and goodness and holiness, and on the other, lies and evil and depravity. It is misleading to call the one angelic and the other satanic, because in many traditions there are angels of darkness as well as angels of light, so here let us take "divine" for the one and "demonic" for the other.

I do not know of any way to write about certain of the onslaughts of fury, of craving for the unlovely, of hubris, of vindictiveness, except in the traditional figurative language that speaks of demonic powers of darkness arrayed against divine powers of light. Reducing these to psychological energies does not do justice to their significance as ultimate evils. Neither does it allow for our pervasive sense of being invaded. The metaphysical status of the invaders is not at issue here; we can deal with that question in any way we please. What matters, and matters supremely, is first the objective difference between the divine and the demonic, a difference that is not merely in the eye of the beholder but is in their essential natures, and second, that neither is impotent. Both of them lure and drive us, and both seem to have an impish sense of humor, notably in the timing of their invasions. Our labor for holiness and against depravity, for good and against evil, is only one skirmish in the war between ultimate forces, but it is a decisive one, because there is such a thing as demonic spirituality, as Charles Williams graphically and grippingly portrays in what T. S. Eliot called his "theological thrillers".

• • •

Finally, the novice can expect that his novitiate will end. Either we commit ourselves to a specific way or we abandon the project—remembering that a novitiate that continues forever is in effect an abandonment. Lest there be any doubt, in this context I do not include in "commitment" the formal, though sometimes very emotional, pledges that often we make in adolescence (or earlier or later), as in "joining the church" or "being confirmed", unless they are preceded by a *spiritual* novitiate. A more vivid term than commitment would be "solemn vow", but a vow carries the sense of a verbal promise to do something specific, whereas a commitment—though no less decisive—is more general, so I have chosen to use the latter.

The act of commitment has often been described as a leap in the dark, sometimes as a terrified leap, like getting married or opening a letter when we know that the contents are fateful. Heretofore we have been on the outside, have seen the domain of spirituality from the outside. No matter how thorough our preparation, we cannot know in advance what it will look like from the inside. But once we have gone inside, we are irrevocably changed. Even if later we revoke our commitment, we shall never again be in the position of having always been outside—as once we have sojourned in a foreign country, we can never again be persons who had not lived there. Whether we stay in that country or return to our original homeland, the change is absolute.

Although this change in commitment is more momentous than most, it is comparable to such everyday movements as from one political party or philosophical position or personal status to another, in that there is no answer to the question, "How did the move take place?" The "how" question implies that there is some process by which the change occurs, but in none of these cases is there any *process* of changing. Before the change, probably there was a process of thinking through the alternatives, and afterwards, a process of adapting, but the change itself is irreducible to stages in a process. Partly for this reason, the commitment has also been compared with the suddenness of falling in love: at one instant we are here, at the next, there in a whole new world. Or as I mentioned previously, we go to bed at night in one world, and wake up the next morning in another. We have made the leap without a conscious decision, much less a desperate jump. "How is one to know which things are really of overmastering importance?" asks a character in Dorothy L. Sayers' *Gaudy Night*, and another answers, "We can only know that when they have overmastered us".[11]

It is easier to write or tell of being pursued by the Hound of Heaven until we collapsed from exhaustion, or of feeling the intolerable yearning so that we took the only way of escape, than of our growing slowly to meet the realization that *this* is the way we must go, followed by stepping almost imperceptibly into full commitment. And the dramatic tales are more memorable, more enticing. Unfortunately, we may tacitly require that such excitements must happen to us, and in our disappointment when our experience does not reproduce those, we doubt the authenticity of the leading that we have received. Or worse, we try to manufacture what we assume to be appropriate feelings. This is one of the situations where a spiritual counsellor can be of inestimable value in saving us from a potentially damaging error.

Apparently the timing of the commitment is not under our control, although this appearance may represent nothing more than a deficiency in the records that are available to us. It is clear, however, that we do not change ourselves by fiat; instead, we are changed. To say this is not to detract from the part we play in preparing to be changed: that is what our whole novitiate is about. It is only to say that when the time comes, the change happens to us; it is not something we do.

The commitment may or may not be marked by an action explicitly confirming that the change has taken place, such as submitting to baptism or donning distinctive clothes. That depends upon what we are now committed to—Christianity or Buddhism, Sufism or Judaism, or whatever it may be—and so lies beyond the scope of this book.

When St Paul wrote in a personal letter—not, please note, a theological treatise—that "the fruit of the Spirit is love, joy, peace, longsuffering, gentleness, goodness, faith, meekness, temperance",[12] he was telling only part of the story. In a letter to a different community, he filled in some of the gaps by listing what he himself had already endured in the course of his spiritual life: "in afflictions, in necessities, in distresses, in stripes, in imprisonments, in tumults, in labours, in watchings, in fastings".[13] And if the records are at all accurate, meekness was hardly one of his salient characteristics.

The fruits of spiritual living are as various as the

fruits of the earth: palatable and unpalatable, nourishing to some and poisonous to others, growing wild and growing at all only with the most careful and skilled cultivation. There is nothing like them, yet everything is like them: they have their analogues in the commonplace, but are raised in the spirit to the Nth power. Our feet are rooted in the earth, and our upraised hands play with the stars.

Who are we? We are who we are: human persons, finite and flawed but capable either of becoming what we essentially are or of becoming, ultimately, nothing, not even a drop of water in an eternal sea. Through all our earthly lives we are moving toward utter fulfilment or utter destruction. Nobody knows what happens to us at death, but there are two principal speculations. One is that "the tree lies as it falls", so that a lifelong or deathbed repentance for sins and reaching out to the ultimate is decisive. According to this view, we are damned to nothingness or saved to consummation by our habitual or climatic rebellion against the ultimate or submission to it during this life. The other is that our deficiencies in this life can be remedied in another, a doctrine variously formulated in terms of a purgatory or of reincarnation. Incidentally, both these doctrines emphasize living in the present so that if we have any life following death in this life, we shall be encumbered as little as may be by our inadequacies in this life.

Only this is certain, that if we seek directly love, joy, peace, and so on, we shall not attain them except by luck or accident. It is of their elusive nature that they come when we are attending to something else. If we seek the ultimate, we may be given these fruits, or we may be given turmoil and afflictions and frustrations—or quietness and dullness and "ease in Zion". We might think here of the banquet when Galahad first took his seat at King Arthur's round table, where each of the knights was served what pleased him best. Whether it was the best because it was what he most desired, or because it was what—unexpectedly—would most deeply satisfy him, we are not told.

EPILOGUE

I have discovered that all the unhappiness of men arises from one single fact, that they cannot stay quietly in their own chamber.

Blaise Pascal
Pensées

EPILOGUE

Il n'y a qu'une tristesse, c'est de n'être pas des saints. [There is only one sorrow, not to be of the saints.]

Léon Bloy

What does it mean, "to be of the saints"? Many years ago I began collecting descriptions not of particular saints, but of what characterizes sanctity. The notebook in which I recorded them has long since disappeared, and I remember only two. The first is from Ignazio Silone's *Bread and Wine*; the statement is attributed to a student in late adolescence.

If the prospect of being displayed on altars after one's death, and being prayed to and worshiped by a lot of unknown people, mostly ugly old ladies, were not very unpleasant, I should like to be a saint. I should not like to live according to circumstances, environment, and material expedience, but I should like, ignoring the consequences, in every hour of my life to live and struggle for that which seems to me to be right and good.[1]

The second is from Charles Morgan's *The Fountain*, and is made by a man convalescing after being grievously wounded in battle. One sentence from it I have quoted earlier.

"The arrogance, the delusion that I have found it hardest to overcome . . . is our belief that we are entitled to first place until we have discovered in our own experience something that transcends us. So we set up idols, our country, our creed, our art, our beloved one, what you will, and pour all our spiritual possessions into the idol's lap. . . . Except to the gods we make out of our experience or dreams we will not kneel down. But the true saint and philosopher," Narwitz concluded in a tone not of assertion but of longing, "is he who can kneel without an image because he sees himself in a second place absolutely, and to kneel is an inward necessity to him. Fate cannot touch such a man—or, rather, though it rend his mind and body, it cannot affect him."[2]

Later he says,

> "Knowledge is static, a stone in the stream,
> but wonder is the stream itself—in common
> men a trickle clouded by doubt, in poets and
> saints a sparkling rivulet, in God a mighty
> river, bearing the whole commerce of the
> divine mind. Is it not true that, even on earth,
> as knowledge increases, wonder deepens?"[3]

In the first quotation, commitment and action are central; in the second, submission and invulnerability; in the third, knowledge and wonder. Yet they fit together, and what brings those who are "of the saints" together is their giving of themselves absolutely, and (although this is apparent only in the context of the stories as wholes from which these quotations are taken) an absolute patience that undergirds even their impetuous actions. Consequently they are integrated. They are whole persons, all of a piece. And because what they have given themsleves to is ultimate good in the one case, and the ultimately holy in the other, they also have integrity.

Being "*of* the saints" does not mean being a saint. Especially it does not mean being perfect. I have played with a fantasy of an assemblage in a heaven when the news comes of an official canonization, and the consternation of Francis or Teresa or Augustine or Jeanne or Thomas when they are singled out. "No! Not me! How ridiculous!!" What had they done to deserve that honor? Nothing—except the work they were called to do. They did, of course, take the trouble to discern *what* they were called to do, and they kept at it come hell and high water. Their struggles were intense and manifold; their inadequacies were glaring; their sins were pervasive. And they knew it.

We who are "of the saints" belong with them from our tentative beginnings to our culmination, as a child belongs within its family, not because of our achievements but because of our common commitment. "It is not what you are or what you have been that God sees with his all-merciful eyes, but what you desire to be".[4] And all the others who are of the saints companion us constantly even—if not especially—when we are not aware of their presence. There is a tale, whose source I cannot locate, of a man who, at the end of his life, reproaches God for having forsaken him in his adversities. "Look across the desert sands where you travelled", God replies, "and you will see not only your own footprints, but also mine beside yours". "But", says the man, "there are those long stretches with only one set of tracks. Why did you leave me then?" And God smiles. "That is where I was carrying you".

"There is only one sorrow"—only one that is beyond consolation—and that is to have no ultimate meaning or significance or place in the universe, and hence no ultimate companionship, which is to say, "not to be of the saints".

NOTES

Prologue
1. Montgomery, "What Is Prayer?" in *Poetical Works*, 412.
2. Lewis, *An Experiment in Criticism*.
3. Morgan, *The Burning Glass*, xxiv.

Chapter One   The Awakening
1. Bonnet and Gouley, *Les ermites*, 156. My translation.
2. Augustine, *Confessions*, vii, 10.
3. Hebrews 5:14.
4. Williams, *The Image of the City*, xliv.
5. Chesterton, "A Prayer in Darkness."

Chapter Two   Under the Aspect of Eternity
1. Morgan, *The Fountain*, 333.
2. Lewis, *An Experiment in Criticism*, 128.
3. Morgan, *Sparkenbroke*, 283.
4. Kierkegaard, *The Sickness unto Death*, xix, 19. I have paraphrased Lowrie's translation.
5. Morgan, *The Voyage*, 14–15, passim.
6. Chesterton, *Varied Types*, 61.

Chapter Three   Approaching the Ultimate
1. Morgan, *The Voyage*, 227.
2. Deuteronomy 6:16.
3. Morgan, *Reflections in a Mirror: Second Series*, 92–93.

4. Ibid., 91.
5. Sayers, *Creed or Chaos?*, 40.
6. Williams, *He Came Down from Heaven*, 25.
7. Aron, *The Jewish Jesus*, 32.
8. Ibid., 33–34.
9. *The Cloud of Unknowing*, 100.
10. Williams, *The Descent of the Dove*, 32.

Chapter Four   Ways of Praying
1. Wordsworth, "Ode on Intimations of Immortality".
2. MacDonald, *Unspoken Sermons*, 177–178.
3. Cf. Holmes, *A History of Christian Spirituality*, 76–77.
4. Cf. Morgan, *The Writer and His World*, 14, 50; and *Sparkenbroke*, 46–48.
5. Cf. Shideler, *The Theology of Romantic Love*, 24–28.
6. All in this paragraph: *The Book of Common Prayer*.
7. Saint Patrick's Hymn.
8. Carmichael, *Celtic Invocations*, 45.
9. Psalm 43:3.
10. Johnson, *God's Trombones*, 13.
11. All in this paragraph: *The Book of Common Prayer*.
12. Williams, *He Came Down from Heaven*, Chapter IV.
13. Williams, *Descent into Hell*, Chapter Six, with an important note in his Introduction to *The Letters of Evelyn Underhill*, 21.
14. Williams, *Descent into Hell*, 98.
15. Byrne, *The Wind Bloweth*, 391.
16. *The Book of Common Prayer*.
17. Aron, *The Jewish Jesus*, 32.
18. *The Book of Common Prayer*: the Te Deum.
19. Sitwell, *Collected Poems*, preface, 1.

20. Whitman, "When Lilacs Last in the Dooryard Bloom'd."
21. Federov, *A Treasury of Russian Spirituality*, 283–345.

Chapter Five   Enablements of Prayer
1. Richter, *The New Yorker*, August 23, 1969, p. 27.
2. Lewis, Introduction to Saint Athanasius' *The Incarnation of the Word of God*, 10.
3. Augustine, *Confessions*, X, xxxiii.
4. Williams, *The Place of the Lion*, 187.
5. All in this paragraph: *The Book of Common Prayer.*
6. Williams, *The English Poetic Mind*, 116–117.
7. Lewis, *The Weight of Glory*, 26.
8. Warner, *The Crossing Fee*, 263–264.
9. Crispin, *Frequent Hearses*, 150.

Chapter Six   Impediments to Prayer
1. Taylor, Jeremy. *Life of Christ*, Part I, §2, ¶27, p. 143.
2. Isaiah 28:16.
3. Teresa of Avila, *Life*, 211.
4. Notably Mary Douglas, *Purity and Danger.*
5. Chesterton, *Orthodoxy*, 11.
6. Morgan, *The Burning Glass*, xxiv.
7. Sayers, *Creed or Chaos?* 63–85.
8. Ibid., 78.
9. Ibid., 77.
10. Ibid., 78.
11. Ibid., 82.
12. Sayers, Notes on Dante's *Purgatory*, 209.
13. Sayers, *Creed or Chaos?*, 66.
14. *The Cloud of Unknowing*, 94.
15. Williams, *The Forgiveness of Sins*, 164.

16. Williams, *Religion and Love in Dante*, 3.
17. Morgan, *Liberties of the Mind*, 50–51.
18. Ibid., 47.
19. Cf. Williams, *Witchcraft, War in Heaven; Many Dimensions; All Hallows' Eve*, and Shideler, "The Mystic, the Psychic, and the Magician".
20. Williams, *The Forgiveness of Sins*, 166.
21. Lewis, *Letters to Malcolm*, 28.
22. Heard, *Ten Questions on Prayer*, 23–25.
23. Morgan, *Reflections in a Mirror: Second Series*, 95.
24. Morgan, *The Flashing Stream*, 24.
25. Ibid., 16–17.,
26. Lewis, *The Screwtape Letters*.
27. Morgan, *The Flashing Stream*, 17.

Chapter Seven   The Life of the Mind
1. Chesterton, *Orthodoxy*, 31–32.
2. Lewis, *Till We Have Faces*, 50.
3. Brooke, *How to Meditate without Leaving the World*.
4. Shideler, *Consciousness of Battle*, 69–70.
5. Eliot, Introduction to Pascal's *Pensées*, xv.
6. Williams, *Rochester*, 239.
7. Teresa of Avila, *Life*, 80.
8. II Kings 5:1–14.
9. Williams, *Descent into Hell*, 174.

Chapter Eight   The Life of Action
1. Williams, *The Figure of Beatrice*, 40.
2. Morgan, *The Judge's Story*, 190.
3. Morgan, *The Writer and His World*, 40.
4. Lewis, "Williams and the Arthuriad", in *Arthurian Torso*, 142.
5. Morgan, *Reflections in a Mirror: First Series*, 131.
6. Houselander, *The Reed of God*, 30.

7. Williams, "Thomas Cranmer of Canterbury," 40.
8. Astley, *The Oxford Dictionary of Quotations*, 2d ed., 21.
9. Quoist, *Prayers*, 66.
10. *The Cloud of Unknowing*, 53.
11. Fortunato, *Embracing the Exile*.
12. Matthew 7:20.

Chapter Nine   The Life of Contemplation
1. Bonnet and Gouley, *Les ermites*.
2. Maritain, *Adventures in Grace*, 318.
3. Ibid., 313.
4. Bottome, *Survival*, 278.
5. Chesterton, *Orthodoxy*, 68.
6. Morgan, *The River Line*, 86.
7. Godden, *In This House of Brede*, 228.
8. McNamara, *Earthy Mysticism*.
9. Lewis, *Surprised by Joy*, 214.
10. Ibid., 202.
11. Sayers, *Gaudy Night*, 37.
12. Galatians 5:22–23.
13. II Corinthians 6:4–5.

Epilogue
1. Silone, *Bread and Wine*, 20.
2. Morgan, *The Fountain*, 333.
3. Ibid., 383.
4. *The Cloud of Unknowing*, 146.

REFERENCES

This list includes material that is quoted or referred to in the text as well as other material that has been of special value to me during my own spiritual journey, and that I most often recommend to others. It does not include the many books, articles, and stories that I have found invaluable, but only as background or supplementary resources. An extensive bibliography of classic works on spirituality can be found in Evelyn Underhill's *Mysticism* (see below), and of more recent works as well in Morton T. Kelsey's *Companions on the Inner Way: The Art of Spiritual Guidance* (New York: Crossroad, 1983).

Allingham, Margery. *The Tiger in the Smoke*. London: Chatto & Windus, 1952.

Anderson, J. Redwood. *Transvaluations*. London: Oxford University Press, 1932.

Anonymous. *The Cloud of Unknowing*. Ed. William Johnston. Garden City, N.Y.: Image Books, 1973.

Aron, Robert. *The Jewish Jesus*. Trans. Agnes H. Forsyth and Anne-Marie de Commaille, and in collaboration with Horace T. Allen, Jr. Maryknoll, N.Y.: Orbis Books, 1971.

Asch, Sholem. *The Apostle*. Trans. Maurice Samuel. New York: Books, Inc., 1943.

Asimov, Isaac. "Profession". *Astounding Science Fiction* LIX (no. 5, July 1957).

Astley, Sir Jacob. *The Oxford Dictionary of Quotations*. 2d ed. London: Oxford University Press, 1955.

Augustine of Hippo. *The Confessions of St Augustine*. Trans. F. J. Sheed. New York: Sheed & Ward, 1943.

Bloy, Léon. Quoted in Maritain, q.v.

Bonnet, Serge, and Gouley, Bernard. *Les ermites*. Paris: Fayard, 1980.

The Book of Common Prayer of the Protestant Episcopal Church. Greenwich, Conn.: Seabury Press, 1928.

Bottome, Phyllis. *Survival*. Boston: Little, Brown & Company, 1943.

Brooke, Avery. *How to Meditate without Leaving the World*. Noroton, Conn.: Vineyard Books, 1975.

Buchan, John. *Mountain Meadow*. New York: The Literary Guild of America, 1940.

Byrne, Donn. *The Wind Bloweth*. New York: The Century Company, 1922.

Carmichael, Alexander. *Celtic Invocations*. Noroton, Conn.: Vincyard Books, 1972.

[Charles, Elizabeth Rundle]. *Chronicles of the Schönberg-Cotta Family*. New York: T. Nelson & Sons, 1865.

Chesterton, G. K. *The Man Who Was Thursday: A Nightmare*. New York: Dodd, Mead & Company, 1908.
——. *Orthodoxy*. London: The Bodley Head, no date. First published in 1908.
——. "A Prayer in Darkness." *Modern American Poetry, Modern British Poetry*. Ed. Louis Untermeyer. New York: Harcourt, Brace and Company, 1930.
——. *Varied Types*. New York: Dodd, Mead & Company, 1921.

Coleridge, Samuel Taylor. "Dejection: An Ode." *Oxford Book of English Verse*. Ed. Charles Williams. London: Victor Gollancz Ltd., 1935.

Crispin, Edmund [Bruce Montgomery]. *Frequent Hearses*. Penguin Books, 1958.

Douglas, Mary. *Purity and Danger: An Analysis of Concepts of Pollution and Taboo*. London: Routledge and Kegan Paul, 1966.

Eliot, T. S. Introduction to *Pascal's Pensées*. Translator not identified. New York: E. P. Dutton & Co., 1958.

Federov, G. P., ed. *A Treasury of Russian Spirituality*. New York: Harper and Row, 1965.

Fortunato, John E. *Embracing the Exile: Spiritual Journeys of Gay Christians*. New York: The Seabury Press, 1982.

Fourez, Gerard, S. J. *Sacraments and Passages: Celebrating the Tensions of Modern Life*. Notre Dame, Indiana: Ave Maria Press, 1983.

Frankl, Viktor E. *Man's Search for Meaning*. Trans. Ilse Lasch. New York: Washington Square Press, 1963.

Godden, Rumer. *In This House of Brede*. New York: The Viking Press, 1969.

Hammarskjöld, Dag. *Markings*. Trans. Leif Sjöberg and W. H. Auden. New York: Alfred A. Knopf, 1964.

Heard, Gerald. *Ten Questions on Prayer*. Wallingford, Pa.: Pendle Hill Pamphlet, 1951.

Henderson, Zenna. *The People: No Different Flesh*. New York: Avon Books, 1967.

—— *Pilgrimage*. New York: Avon Books, 1961.

Holmes, Urban T. III. *A History of Christian Spiritu-*

ality: An Analytical Introduction. New York: The Seabury Press, 1981.

Houselander, Caryll. *The Reed of God*. New York: Arena Lettres, 1978.

John of the Cross, St. *Dark Night of the Soul*. Ed. and trans. E. Allison Peers. Garden City, N.Y.: Image Books, 1959.

Johnson, James Weldon. *God's Trombones*. New York: The Viking Press, 1932.

Julian of Norwich. *Revelations of Divine Love*. Ed. Dom Roger Hudleston, O.S.B. London: Burns Oates, 1952.

Juster, Norton. *The Dot and the Line*. New York: Random House, 1963.

Keating, Thomas; Pennington, Basil; and Clarke, Thomas E. *Finding Grace at the Center*. Still River, Mass.: Saint Bede Publications, 1978.

Kerr, Walter. *The Decline of Pleasure*. New York: Simon & Schuster, 1962.

Kierkegaard, Søren. *The Sickness unto Death*. Trans. Walter Lowrie. Princeton, N.J.: The Princeton University Press, 1941.

Kipling, Rudyard. "The Obedient." *Rudyard Kipling's Verse: Inclusive Edition, 1885–1932*. New York: Doubleday, Doran & Company, 1938.

———. "The Palace." Ibid.

Lewis, C. S. *The Abolition of Man*. New York: The Macmillan Publishing Company, 1947.

———. Introduction to Athanasius. *The Incarnation of the Word of God*. Trans. a religious of C.S.M.V., S.Th. New York: The Macmillan Publishing Company, 1946.

——. *The Discarded Image*. Cambridge: Cambridge University Press, 1964.

——. *An Experiment in Criticism*. Cambridge: Cambridge University Press, 1961.

——. *The Great Divorce*. New York: The Macmillan Company, 1946.

——. *Letters to Malcolm: Chiefly on Prayer*. London: Geoffrey Bles, 1964.

——. *Out of the Silent Planet*. New York: The Macmillan Company, 1944.

——. *Perelandra*. The New York: The Macmillan Company, 1944.

——. *The Screwtape Letters*. New York: The Macmillan Company, 1943.

——. *Surprised by Joy*. London: Geoffrey Bles, 1955.

——. *Till We Have Faces*. New York: Harcourt, Brace and Company, 1956.

——. *The Weight of Glory and Other Addresses*. New York: The Macmillan Company, 1949.

MacDonald, George. *Unspoken Sermons*. London: Alexander Strahan, 1867.

Maritain, Raïssa. *We Have Been Friends Together* and *Adventures in Grace*. Trans. Julie Kernan. Garden City, N.Y.: Image Books, 1961.

McNamara, William. *Earthy Mysticism*. New York: Crossroad, 1983.

Mew, Charlotte. "Madeleine in Church." *Collected Poems of Charlotte Mew*. London: Gerald Duckworth & Company, 1953.

Montgomery, James. *The Poetical Works of James Montgomery*. Edinburgh: Gall & Inglis, 1870.

Morgan, Charles. *The Burning Glass: A Play*. London: Macmillan & Co., Ltd., 1954.

———. *The Flashing Stream*. London: Macmillan & Co., Ltd., 1953.

———. *The Fountain*. New York: Alfred A. Knopf, 1932.

———. *The Judge's Story*. London: Macmillan & Co., Ltd., 1958.

———. *Liberties of the Mind*. London: Macmillan & Co., Ltd., 1952.

———. *Reflections in a Mirror, First Series*. London: Macmillan & Co., Ltd., 1944.

———. *Reflections in a Mirror, Second Series*. London: Macmillan & Co., Ltd., 1947.

———. *The River Line*. London: Macmillan & Co., Ltd., 1959.

———. *Sparkenbroke*. London: Macmillan & Co., Ltd., 1936.

———. *The Voyage*. London: Macmillan & Co., Ltd., 1940.

———. *The Writer and His World*. London: Macmillan & Co., Ltd., 1961.

Ossorio, Peter G. *The Behavior of Persons*. Book in preparation.

———. *Clinical Topics* (LRI Report No. 11). Whittier, Calif. and Boulder, Colo.: Linguistic Research Institute, 1976.

———. *Positive Health and Transcendental Theories* (LRI Report No. 13). Whittier, Calif. and Boulder, Colo.: Linguistic Research Institute, 1977.

———. *Religion without Doctrine* (LRI Report No. 19). Boulder, Colo.: Linguistic Research Institute, 1978.

———. *"What Actually Happens"*. Columbia, S.C.: University of South Carolina Press, 1978.

Patrick, St. "St Patrick's Hymn." *The Hymnal of the*

251

Protestant Episcopal Church in the United States of America. New York: The Church Pension Fund, 1940.

Peguy, Charles. *God Speaks: Religious Poetry*. Trans. Julian Green. New York: Pantheon Books, 1945.

Quoist, Michel. *Prayers*. Trans. Agnes M. Forsyth and Anne Marie de Commaille. New York: Sheed and Ward, 1963.

Richter, Mischa. Cartoon in *The New Yorker*, August 23, 1969, p. 27.

Rolland, Romain. *Jean-Christophe*. Trans. Gilbert Cannan. New York: The Modern Library, 1910.

Sayers, Dorothy L. *Creed or Chaos?*. New York: Harcourt, Brace and Company, 1949.

———. "The Devil to Pay." *Four Sacred Plays*. London: Victor Gollancz, 1957.

———. *Gaudy Night*. New York: Harper & Brothers, 1936.

———. *The Man Born to be King* New York: Harper & Brothers, 1943.

———. *The Mind of the Maker*. New York: Harcourt, Brace and Company, 1941.

———. Notes on Dante's *Purgatory*. Penguin Books, 1955.

Schachter-Shalomi, Zalman, and Gropman, Donald. *The First Step: A Guide to the New Jewish Spirit*. New York: Bantam Books, 1983.

Schmemann, Alexander. *For the Life of the World*. New York: National Student Christian Federation, 1963.

Schreiner, Olive. *Dreams*. "Little Blue Book No. 29." Girard, Kansas: Haldeman-Julius Company, no date.

Shideler, Mary McDermott. *Consciousness of Battle*.

Grand Rapids, Mich.: Wm. B. Eerdmans Publishing Company, 1969.

—— "The Mystic, the Psychic, and the Magician." *Dialog, 16 (No. 2, Spring 1977).*

——. *The Theology of Romantic Love.* New York: Harper & Brothers, 1962.

Silone, Ignazio. *Bread and Wine.* Trans. Gwenda David and Eric Mosbacher. New York: Harper & Brothers, 1937.

Sitwell, Edith. "Some Notes on My Own Poetry." *Collected Poems of Edith Sitwell.* New York: The Vanguard Press, 1954.

Taylor, Jeremy. *Life of Christ.* Vol. 2, *The Whole Works of the Right Rev. Jeremy Taylor, D.D.* Ed. the Right Rev. Reginald Heber, D.D. London: Longman, Brown, Green, & Longmans, 1847.

Taylor, John V. *The Primal Vision.* Philadelphia: The Fortress Press, 1964.

Teresa of Avila. *Life.* Vol. 1, *Saint Teresa's Complete Works.* Ed. and trans. E. Allison Peers. London: Sheed and Ward, 1963.

Thompson, Francis. "The Hound of Heaven." *Modern American Poetry, Modern British Poetry.* Ed. Louis Untermeyer. N.Y.: Harcourt, Brace and Company, 1930.

——. "In No Strange Land." Ibid.

Tolkien, J. R. R. *The Lord of the Rings.* London: George Allen & Unwin Ltd., 1955.

Underhill, Evelyn. *The Letters of Evelyn Underhill.* Ed. Charles Williams. London: Longmans, Green and Company, 1943.

——. *Mysticism.* London: Methuen & Company, 1930. First published in 1911.

Vlastos, Gregory. *The Religious Way*. New York: The Womans Press, 1934.

Warner, Esther [Esther Warner Dendel]. *The Crossing Fee*. Boston: Houghton Mifflin Company, 1968.

——. *Seven Days to Lomaland*. New York: Pyramid Books, 1967.

Whitman, Walt. *Leaves of Grass*. New York: The Modern Library, 1921.

Williams, Charles. *All Hallows' Eve*. London: Faber & Faber Ltd., 1945.

——. *Descent into Hell*. London: Faber & Faber Ltd., 1937.

——. *The Descent of the Dove*. London: Faber & Faber Ltd., 1939.

——. *The English Poetic Mind*. London: Oxford University Press, 1932.

——. *The Figure of Beatrice*. London: Faber & Faber Ltd., 1938.

——. *Flecker of Dean Close*. London: The Canterbury Press, 1946.

——. *He Came Down from Heaven* (including *The Forgiveness of Sins*). London: Faber & Faber Ltd., 1940.

——. "Il ben dell' Intelletto," in *Time and Tide* (London) 23 (no. 21, May 23, 1942).

——. *The Image of the City and Other Essays*. Edited by Anne Ridler. London: Oxford University Press, 1958.

——. *Many Dimensions*. London: Faber & Faber Ltd., 1933.

——. *The Place of the Lion*. London: Faber & Faber Ltd., 1931.

——. *Religion and Love in Dante*. London: The Dacre Press, 1941.

———. *Rochester*. London: Arthur Barker, 1935.

———. "Thomas Cranmer of Canterbury." *Collected Plays*. London: Oxford University Press, 1963.

———. *War in Heaven*. London: Faber & Faber Ltd., 1930.

———. *Witchcraft*. London: Faber & Faber Ltd., 1941.

——— and Lewis, C. S. *Arthurian Torso*. London: Oxford University Press, 1948.

ABOUT THE AUTHOR

Mary McDermott Shideler is a past president of the American Theological Society (Midwest Division). An authority on British authors Charles Williams and Charles Morgan, she is also the author of six books and over forty articles as well as a contributor to *The Christian Century*, *The Review Of Books and Religion*, and other theological publications.

A graduate of Swarthmore College, Mary Shideler makes her home outside Boulder, Colorado, high in the Rocky Mountains.